# From the Deck
## of
# Your Own Yacht

**AT THE QUAY.**

*Barrie Neilson*

# From the Deck of Your Own Yacht

The start of flotilla sailing
and what happened next
in the Ionian Sea

FloMo Publishing

First published in 2009

British Library Cataloguing in Publication Data

A catalogue record for this book is available from the British Library.

ISBN 978 0 9561870 0 0

Published by
FloMo Publishing
87 South Road
Oundle
Peterborough PE8 4BP
UK
email: flomo_books@btinternet.com

Designed and produced by
Keyword Ltd
2 Denford Ash Cottages
Denford
Kettering
Northants NN14 4BW
Tel: 01832 734425
email: wadams1907@aol.com

Printed and bound in the Czech Republic

*Title page* Skopelos in the Sporades, 1980. *YCA*

# Acknowledgements

Grateful thanks to: Eric Richardson of YCA and Barrie Neilson of Sailing Holidays, who told me the stories, gave me access to their companies' archives and patiently answered many e-mails; John Hooker, Doug Kennett, Ian Meikle, Bill and Ann Melville, Janet Welch and G. W., who shared their memories and their photos; Nigel and Angie Blackman, David Brooke-Smith, Scott Brown and Mike Cox, who worked on early flotillas and remember the excitement of those days; Matt West, who made some essential introductions, as well as to all those at Sunsail who helped me make extra trips to the Mediterranean for my research; Frances Illingworth, for her expertise in translation from Greek; Nicky, Katherine, Nick, and Bernard, for their anchor-work; and to my many friends working in tavernas and restaurants, some but not all quoted here, whose hospitality over the years gave me the idea for this book.

In addition to the archives and reminiscences that I mention above, I have quoted from three books:

• Ernle Bradford's *Companion Guide to the Greek Islands* was published in 1963, and though it is not a pilot book it was written by someone who knew the islands as a small-boat sailor.

• Hammond Innes's *Sea and Islands* was published in 1967, though he visited the Ionian in 1965. The book deals with voyages and races in his yacht *Mary Deare*.

• Lawrence Durrell's *The Greek Islands*, published in 1978, aimed to be a personal guide to the area, so is quirkier and more interesting than most straightforward works for tourists.

I have also quoted from Joan Gould's article 'Sailing the Wine-Dark Seas', originally published in the *New York Times*.

The extracts from these works are intended to provide a fleeting glimpse of some of the places before the flotillas started to visit. For simplicity, the quotations are attributed just to the writers, but they are always from the works listed here. Where these authors used different spelling for place names I have maintained them in the quotations.

Many of the photographs originally appeared in the brochures of flotilla companies, and are used here by kind permission of YCA, Sailingholidays.com or Sunsail. Others were sent to me by the individuals listed and thanked elsewhere in the acknowledgements. Some of the YCA brochures printed credits to individuals who contributed pictures: I have repeated these credits and send my best wishes to anyone who finds their holiday snaps from 30 years ago reproduced here.

# Contents

# *Introduction*

Nowadays, flotilla sailing seems such an obvious idea. But when in April 1974 the very first group of eleven boats set off from Aegina in the Saronic Gulf, no one involved had any idea that they were at the beginning of something that would grow so big. In any case, the whole notion almost ended within a few weeks when Greece went to war.

By the mid-1970s whole regions of the Mediterranean had been changed, not always for the better, by the advent of package flights. Along with the holiday-making families from tour companies came the backpackers and island-hoppers. Many of the islands of Greece became the territory of the kind of visitor who thought that sleeping on the beach, partying late into the night and leaving a trail of empty beer-cans was an appropriate response to the relative simplicity of the local lifestyle and the real hospitality of the people.

Some of the islands were off the beaten track, though. In 1976 an advertisement referred to 'the beautiful undiscovered Ionian Islands'. H. M.

Denham's *Ionian Islands to Greece*, revised in 1978, says

'Sivota Bay lies at the head of a narrow wooded inlet with natural all-round shelter and perfect solitude in most attractive surroundings. A taverna and one or two farmsteads are near the shore.'

An island-hopping guide published in 1980 said

'Outside of July and August the typical tourist in Ithaca has his Homer under his arm and his hiking shoes on his feet.'

By the time that last sentence was published a new type of holiday had been invented. It would introduce thousands of people to relatively inaccessible areas and create a type of visitor industry that would help to increase the prosperity of the towns and villages while respecting their essential character. Flotilla sailing was coming.

Together with the flotilla boats and individual

*Left* A Snapdragon arriving at Hydra in 1978. *YCA*

*Right* Alonisos village. *C. Hannah*

charters came private yachts from all over Europe, attracted by the improved harbours and profusion of quiet anchorages. Princes and princesses on honeymoon shared swimming anchorages with families enjoying their first experience of taking charge of a small sailing boat. Small beach cafés became thriving restaurants, abandoned houses in villages were renovated and a whole new tourism structure sprang up, ashore and afloat.

Despite these changes, taxi-drivers in the Ionian still stop on the road to buy fish or just to point out the best view between the mountains, and the fishermen still have the most sheltered spots in the harbours – as they should. Some of the bigger villages found themselves with villas and small hotels dedicated to land-based visitors attracted by the improved transport links, and one or two now have a row of restaurants the length of a new quay, but Greek law has kept a brake on the size and style of building. A good friend who has a successful restaurant is proud that he has built a house on the edge of town with a vegetable garden and olive trees. He and his wife work hard all summer, and their sons (the eldest one already works for a high-tech engineering firm in Germany) wait at table in the evenings. From October to Easter he is determined that he and his family can continue to experience the lifestyle of his own parents, farming and fishing.

One of the attractions of any part of Greece is the wealth of history and myth. A first landfall by small boat on Ithaca leads inevitably to thoughts of Odysseus. This book makes no attempt to deal with antiquity, because two connected things are certain: the very fact that you are holding it shows that you have been captured by the spirit of the islands, and you already know Rod Heikell's pilot books, which are much more than just guides to harbours.

Authors find it difficult to write about the Ionian without quoting Cavafy's poem 'Ithaca.' I shall resist the temptation, but set it as your homework. Make a point of finding it. You may not have the experience of having it read to you in Greek, with translation and explanation, one evening in a bay on Meganisi by a Greek-American on the next boat, but the poem will not disappoint you.

Sivota, Levkas. In 1985 the water was still lapping up to the buildings. *Sailing Holidays*

# Part 1
# The Start of the Flotillas

## 1
## The idea

Eric Richardson denies being the father of flotilla sailing, saying he just 'tripped over the concept'. It was certainly his energy that developed it. Within a couple of years the outline idea, which much of the yachting industry rejected, had become a success that other companies were eager to join.

Eric had worked in the holiday and airline business all his life. Clarksons, one of the very first charter-flight companies, had been formed to arrange the travel for the executives of the parent ship-broking companies and other international businesses. This developed into offering the public short trips and holidays to the Dutch bulb-fields and the Rhine valley. Vikings and Dakotas and a few Viscounts were chartered from all the commercial airfields in the UK; they would just fly to the destination and fly back in the evening. Eric moved to other charter airlines, running trooping flights before the decision was made for the RAF to take over this work. A lot of the companies failed at this point, including the one Eric was with, and

Eric Richardson in conference in 1973. *Eric Richardson*

he started by himself chartering aircraft for people who wanted to visit friends in the USA or Canada.

With the change of regulations about such flights, more and more companies were joining in, and in the early 1970s Eric was looking for another niche market. As a sailor himself he had already realised that UK sailors would love to be able to sail in the sun, and was researching the possibility of packaged self-sail holidays in the Mediterranean.

The impetus to look seriously at a particular area came when Marjorie Sharp, who worked for Eric, was at a health farm. She was in a steam cabinet (think *Thunderball*, where Bond traps a baddy in one), and in the next cabinet was the wife of a businessman, living in Greece, who wanted to start a yacht charter business.

As a result of that conversation Eric was invited to Greece, and the steam-cabinet lady and her husband showed him round and introduced him to lots of people. Eric's host wanted to build up a business offering large boats with professional crews, so the plans of the two men did not overlap, but in the spring of 1973 Eric was touring the Saronic Gulf and was 'enchanted' by what he saw.

A possible direction would have been just to offer small yachts for charter. However, the potential size of what we should now call the 'bare-boat' market seemed uncertain, and supporting the charterers would have presented considerable problems.

Nowadays a whole infrastructure exists to support the sailor who takes an unfamiliar boat for a week or two, possibly with a young family on board. Very detailed pilot books give guidance about harbours and coves. In every harbour there are people familiar with the way yachts moor, plenty of bollards or rings to use, and probably other people on boats who might take a shore-line. In the bigger towns there are chandleries, as well as boat engineers and sailmakers. The lead-crews of flotillas can usually be persuaded, once their charges are safely in and for the cost of a few drinks, to help with running repairs.

None of this was the case in the early 1970s, so it was unlikely that any but the most confident visitors would take a bare-boat for a short period.

Yachtsmen from abroad did visit Greece, of course. Ernle Bradford sailed the area in the 1950s

The offices where the first flotillas were organised. Quill Travel Services was Eric's company, which took care of the flights. *Eric Richardson*

Marjorie Sharp (holding the glass). After a chance conversation Marjorie made the introduction that took Eric to the Saronic Gulf on his first survey. Half a dozen years later she was shown in the YCA brochure for 1978 dining aboard a flotilla yacht at Vathi on Ithaca. *C. Head*

and his *Companion Guide to the Greek Islands* and *Ulysses Found* were published in the early '60s. Captain H. M. Denham's sea-guides were first published in the mid-'60s, while Hammond Innes's *Sea and Islands* describes his extended cruises.

These were people sailing their own boats, familiar with the equipment, and with crews who, however young, had become accustomed to life on board. By actually arriving in Greek waters they had proved their expertise. Eric was thinking of providing a holiday that would extend the sailing experience of those who took part: a bigger boat, or further offshore, or in better weather. Many of them would be dinghy sailors, with excellent boat-handling skills but little background in anchoring or mooring.

The idea of sailing as a mini-fleet came to him while sitting on a rock in Poros harbour. The name 'flotilla sailing' was conceived later when he wrote the first brochure. The Saronic Gulf seemed an ideal location, particularly because flights to Athens were easily available.

*A*mong the many yachtsmen who have contributed their experiences to this book was Doug Kennett, who took his young family on a one-year educational voyage under sail from the UK and visited the Ionian in 1976:

'In those days one needed a smattering of Greek to get by! However, upon our arrival in Greece, as we approached the deserted quay at Argostoli, the Customs Official was waiting to take our lines and said in English, "Welcome to Greece." He came on board and chatted for a while whilst the evening meal, prepared by our 12-year-old daughter, filled our 38-foot steel ketch with anticipation.

In the following weeks we visited nearly every port and cove mentioned in Captain H. Denham's *The Ionian Islands* and some other unnamed coves as well. Only once did we not have these remote anchorages to ourselves. What a host of happy memories we have of those crystal-clear waters where you can see the anchor holding in 30 feet of water, see the fish nibble and bite your baited hook, and watch the sun go down behind the islands in a silence only disturbed by birdsong and the mystical music of the variously toned bells around the necks of sheep and goats as the herds led the singing shepherds over the hillside back to the security of a village for the night. The walks to these villages for the bread, feta, local wine, yoghurt and fruit that frequently formed our midday meal were therapeutic in their simplicity, and it was impossible to refuse the glass of ouzo so frequently offered by the locals. How generous and friendly are the rural Greeks.

Hot, high hills or mountains rising from the sea so often give rise to violent, sudden squalls that one needs to have excellent ground tackle and at times even be prepared to make a hasty retreat from what a few moments earlier was a peaceful cove. These squalls were most likely in the afternoon and we aimed to get the shorter passages over by midday, which sometimes gave the added pleasure of seeing the islands slowly unveiled from a still sea as the sea dispersed the morning mist. I never did really understand why a violent squall sometimes shattered the peace of the night as well, but after the first occasion I took the precaution of noting bearings and distances to facilitate escape from the more remote coves whose total desertion had become an attraction for us.'

Sarakiniko Cove, Ithaca, 1976. Doug Kennett writes of a 'long-promised moonlight swim and midnight feast for the younger members of the crew in Sarakiniko Cove. It was a grand, majestic, superb scene with a full, very bright moon bathing the cove in a light so intense it could have been daylight, and a slight swell caused the surf to break gently on the shingle shore.' *Doug Kennett*

# YCA and ²Snappies

The Yacht Cruising Association was established as the first company to offer a chance to 'see the Greek Islands from the deck of your own yacht'.

Why was a commercial venture called an association? One reason was to avoid a pitfall that began to be mentioned as the project started. Eric says:

'Based upon my experience at the time in the tour-operating industry I never considered that there would be a problem with the authorities about bringing in tourists to Greece. This was naive. But foreign sailing clubs were exempt from the regulations we began to learn about.'

One such regulation, which was believed at the time to be the case, was that chartered yachts had to have a Greek skipper. (On the other hand, the super yachts available for charter mainly to US people seemed to have 'foreign' skippers.) It is worth noting that the company that eventually developed into Sailing Holidays was called the Flotilla Sailing Club during much of the 1970s and '80s. A few years after the first flotillas began to operate, a new Greek law required charter boats to sail under the Greek flag. This clarified the requirement without simplifying it: YCA had to set up a 51% Greek company legally owning the yachts.

In addition, the name became a marketing asset as it made the clients feel they were taking part in something more personal than just a summer break, and Joan Gould's article quoted below and written as late as 1982 described the company as having a purely amateur origin. It did actually function as a members' club though: people joined it, and paid an admission fee. Mike Cox says:

'We did a lot of things for them: there were AGMs, reunions, big dinners on the *Hispaniola* on the Thames. We had some great times at the end of each season: there was very much a family or clubby feel to it.'

The friendships made between the flotilla members was something they discovered to be one of the strengths of Eric's idea. Jane Hannah, a hostess in the early days, says, 'There is still a wonderful camaraderie among charterers.'

Eric approached friends in the tour-operating industry to purchase an allocation of flight seats to Athens. An informal contract was made with Stuart Alderman, who managed Wings, for forty seats fortnightly for £26 return on one of their flights.

Eric believes the contract was informal because Stuart didn't have much faith in the success of the project. Possibly he under estimates Stuart, who must have recognised the determination that was already a major style-feature of the young YCA.

In the 1975 brochure this explanation is given of the status of the YCA.

'During 1973 it was decided to form the "Yacht Cruising Association" which is a members club for people who have taken our flotilla cruising holidays abroad. The Association, which is affiliated to the Royal Yachting Association, leases from its members and in some cases owns the yachts that are used for the cruising holidays in this brochure. The travel arrangements are managed by Quill Travel Services Ltd, who are members of the Association of British Travel Agents.'

*This page* Pages from the invitation to the 1976 Reunion Party for members of the YCA. The winning caption for the cartoon at the top was: 'If that's the best you can do to signal "Line Abreast", thank goodness I didn't ask you for "Line Astern".' *YCA*

*Opposite page* Eric's September 1973 letter to Thames Marine confirming the order for the first group of boats. The opening confirms the order, while the conditions agree that the order could be cancelled up to 1 January without penalty, but Eric is sufficiently confident to have also made provisional booking for production space for further boats during the same winter.

The end of the letter was in reply to one in which Peter Simmons had hoped that 'next week will prove favourable for Mediterranean-type photographs taken in the Thames Estuary!' This referred to publicity photographs to be taken for the YCA brochure showing a Snapdragon sailing in the sunshine. His later response to Eric's request for candy-striped awnings on the YCA Boat Show stand was that, after discussion with the stand design consultant, 'I do not really feel that this would be entirely in keeping with the image we are trying to project at the London Show'. In 1973 the vast majority of yachtsmen at the Show would have been looking for a boat with a hard-bitten sou'westered image for butting through British coastal waters. He was 'only too pleased' to agree to all the other publicity suggestions, though.

*Eric Richardson*

## Agenda

- Preliminary Warm Up - Ouzo hour
- Mike Cox's Ionian Lecture- Please assemble on quay in good time.
- Photographic Competition Results.
- Quiet Hour for Poem Reading - All poems to be read personally to Sally at least 48 hours before to ensure suitability.
- Cartoon Captions - [Subject to censure].
- Sporadic Sea Tales.
- Entry of YCA Into Greek Mythology - Lecture by F. Harry. Stow.
- Sardonic Sea Stories.
- The Avon Dinghy's Lament - (YCA Song) to the tune of "You scratch my bottom and I'll scratch yours".

## Cartoons

These cartoons were drawn by YCA member, Pat McLaughlin. Please bring them to the party with your suggestions for suitable captions. Write your caption on the invitation and also, if you dare, your name!

## Invitation

Once again, it is time to splice the YCA Mainbrace. You and your crew are invited to attend the Yard Arm Club at three bells on Friday 26th November. The Yard Arm Club is aboard the "Hispaniola" which is moored on the Thames almost opposite Charing Cross tube station.

Best quality ships biscuits with fresh weevils will be served during the evening and there are bars on the upper deck and bars down below. As is our normal practice, we'll be taking an inventory after you leave.

We now know what we're doing for 1977 (about time too! ) and will be breaking the news gently during the evening.

More new yachts will be added to the fleet so once again we are looking for volunteers to run the Adriatic Gauntlet and help us with the deliveries. There is also a little problem of moving boats around in Greece for our new Ionian adventure which we think you may be able to help us with - Sally's revealing all on the night!

The price of the tickets is £6 each (excluding damage deposit) and we really hope you'll be able to come.

Dress is informal, but gentlemen in Greek skirts will not be piped aboard.

(All bells are in local time)

Mr P Simmonds
Marketing Manager
Thames Marine
T.S.P. (Marine) Limited
Charfleet
Canvey Island, Essex SS8 OPQ           26th September 1973

Dear Mr Simmonds,

Further to your letter of 29th August, I am writing to confirm our
order for 11 Snapdragon 747 yachts which are required for our Greek Island
sailing holidays.

Precise details of colour, sail wardrobe and equipment requirements will be
advised in due course but you may take this letter as confirmation that we
intend to proceed with the plans we outlined to you during my recent visit.

The conditions of this order are that we will pay you a deposit of 10% of
the purchase price and enclosed is our cheque for £4,000 which represents
approximately 10% of the value of this order. We cannot at this stage be
precise as it is not clear what items of equipment we would like to have
included. It is agreed that the purchase price for the yachts will be your

...............................

In the event that this project is unsuccessful you would allow us free
cancellation of this order up to 1st January less a nominal amount to
cover the cost of any clerical work you had undertaken. I will keep
you fully informed about how this project is proceeding and if the
indications are that we should increase the fleet size I understand
that you would be willing to reserve production space sufficient for a
further ten/eleven yachts until the end of January, subject to our giving
you some guide lines by end November. Should this happy situation arise we
would then be granted an additional 2½% discount for the complete order.

I understand that the UK boat holiday operators achieve excellent results
from the London Boat Show. I enquired many months ago and found that there
was no stand space available as they had been over subscribed. I mentioned
to you about the possibility of your being able to distribute our publicity
material from your own stand, but wonder if we could take this a step
further. My idea is that we would take a full colour page in the Boat Show
catalogue. This advertisement would show the "747" and invite people to
look at the boat on the Thames Marine stand. On your stand beside the "747"
you could perhaps have some form of notice saying "Yacht Cruising Associates
choose Snapdragon 747 for their Greek Island Cruising Holidays". To further
draw attention to this boat it could be rigged with the sun awning we would
be using. These would be in candy strips and look very attractive! Please
let me know what you and your publicity people think of this idea. I really
need your comments by this coming Friday because it is at that time we
have to confirm the space order for the Boat Show catalogue. Obviously
supplies of our brochure would be available on the stand.

I am very pleased that we have decided to work with Thames Marine on this
project and hope that this will be the start of a long and friendly
cooperation with you and your company.

Yours sincerely,


Eric Richardson

### Sailing Equipment

20 lb. Main Anchor, Chain, warp and chocks; 20 lb. Kedge Anchor and Warp; Fenders; Boathook; Swimming Ladder; Fuel and Water Funnels; Deck Mop and Scrubber; Ensign; Greek Courtesy Ensign; YCA Burgee; Dinghy, Oars and rowlocks; Bilge Pump; Sheet Winches with top handles; Steering Compass; Necessary Charts and case; Parallel rulers; Navigation Lights; Masthead light; Pulpit, Pushpit; Stanchions and Lifelines; Cockpit Cushions.

### Galley Equipment

Two-burner Gas stove and Grill: Bucket; Dustpan and Brush; Dish Mop and Pan Scourer; Tea Towels (disposable); Sponge; Clothes Pegs; Refuse Bags; 5 sets knives, forks, dessert spoons, teaspoons, cups, saucers, glasses, mugs, tea plates, dinner plates, cereal bowls, egg cups; Butter Dish and Sugar Bowl; 2 jugs; Cruet; Grill pan; 3 saucepans; frying pan; Kettle; Ice box; Wooden spoon; Bread, carving and vegetable knives; Cooking fork; Strainer/Spoon; Frying slice; Tin opener; Corkscrew; Colander; Food containers; Washing-up liquid; Toilet Rolls; Polish, bleach and washing powders.

### Safety Equipment

Buoyancy aids; Children's Harness; Lifebuoy; Warning instrument; Distress flares; Fire extinguishers; Flash light; Batteries and Bulbs; First aid kit.

### Bedding

Blankets; Bag sheets; Foam Pillows, Slips; Air bed (for deck sleeping and swimming).

### Cabin Fittings

Sea Toilet; Freshwater shower; 8-track stereo deck; 240v shaver socket; 'C' shaped dinette for 5 adults.

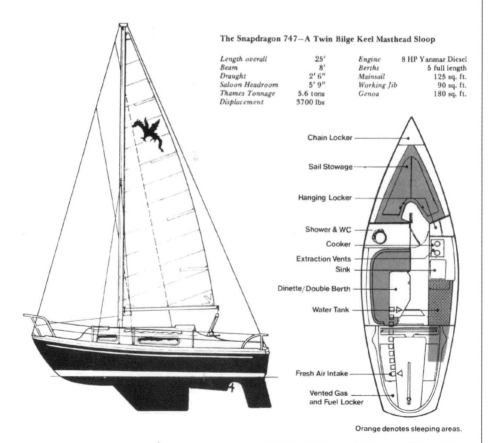

**The Snapdragon 747—A Twin Bilge Keel Masthead Sloop**

| | | | | |
|---|---|---|---|---|
| *Length overall* | 25' | *Engine* | 8 HP Yanmar Diesel |
| *Beam* | 8' | *Berths* | 5 full length |
| *Draught* | 2' 6" | *Mainsail* | 125 sq. ft. |
| *Saloon Headroom* | 5' 9" | *Working Jib* | 90 sq. ft. |
| *Thames Tonnage* | 5.6 tons | *Genoa* | 180 sq. ft. |
| *Displacement* | 3700 lbs | | |

Chain Locker

Sail Stowage

Hanging Locker

Shower & WC

Cooker

Extraction Vents

Sink

Dinette/Double Berth

Water Tank

Fresh Air Intake

Vented Gas and Fuel Locker

Orange denotes sleeping areas.

*Left* Details of the Snapdragons, from the 1973 YCA brochure. The first batch ordered were bilge-keelers, so that if YCA cancelled its order the boats could be sold in the UK market. *YCA*

*Above* A Snapdragon in Greece in the first flotilla season. *YCA*

Several British boat-builders were visited to discuss the project, yacht specifications, prices and delivery dates. They were highly sceptical, and said they were unable to build boats to the necessary schedule. Essentially they didn't think it was a serious idea. Finally Eric was introduced to Ray Walsh of Thames Marine on Canvey Island, the first boat-builder who did not immediately assume he was of unsound mind. In late summer 1973 an order was placed for eleven Snapdragons: ten for the flotilla plus a lead-boat. The deal was that the order could be cancelled by the start of January without penalty. These first boats were to be the bilge-keel version, so that if the project failed to take off Thames Marine would be able to sell them.

# 3
# Marketing and delivery

Writing the first brochure was difficult because this was pioneering tourism. Eric wrote a cruise route based on his limited experience of the area. This leaned heavily on Captain Denham's *Aegean Pilot*, but any plagiarism must have been made up for by the number of copies that the project later caused to be sold. Rod Heikell's cruising guides came much later, of course.

General photographs were not a problem, for even then places en route such as Hydra, Epidavros and Spetsai were well-known and pictures could be obtained from photo libraries, but there were no Snapdragons in Greece. This problem was resolved one cold but relatively sunny afternoon off Canvey Island. Thames Marine provided two boats, and the crew of this very first YCA cruise included bikini-clad au pair Lena, Eric's six-year-old son Bruce and his friend Tony. The main props were Greek salad and wine.

The operation did not go as smoothly as had been hoped, though since the outcome was pictures of Snapdragons sailing in the sun, the day was counted a success. The photographers brought the wrong speed film, though that was later put right. Lena, who was new to sea-life, arrived in high-heels and had forgotten to take her sea-sickness pills. She smiled bravely apart from when her head was over the side.

What was now lacking was a picture to sum up sailing in the Greek islands: a beautiful bay, clear water and just one yacht at anchor. Eric scoured the photo libraries and found just such a shot. Phil

The cover picture of the first YCA brochure. There were no Snapdragons to photograph in Greece, so this sunny scene was photographed off Canvey Island using a Snapdragon borrowed from Thames Marine. *YCA*

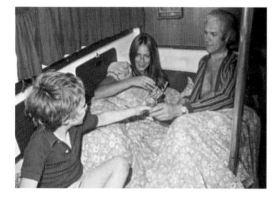

The first flotilla brochure included these pictures of the carefree life aboard a sailing yacht amongst the Greek islands. Again, the photo-shoot took place in the Thames estuary, with a cast of Eric's friends and his young son. *YCA*

For the first brochures this photo library shot was found and captioned 'Inaccessible coves and quiet unspoiled beaches…'. It was not until several years later that the team noticed that the yacht was flying a Majorcan courtesy flag. Of course, the brochure did not claim that the yacht was in Greece… *YCA*

Murphy, who did the design work for the brochure, decided to use this photo full page and it was not until several years later that the team noticed that the yacht was flying a Majorcan courtesy flag.

Of course, the brochure did not claim that the Snapdragons or the yacht were sailing in Greece, but neither did it say it was Canvey Island or Majorca. And the following year there were plenty of real photos to use.

Then as now the London Boat Show in January was the major market-place for such a project. Unfortunately YCA was told that there was no room for them: Eric says he pleaded, but to no avail. The problem may have been that the Show was completely booked up well in advance, or it may have been part of a general lack of enthusiasm from the public faces of yachting for this completely new idea.

The sailing press in general was very cool. One editor said he thought the idea impractical and YCA would be on the rocks in a few weeks. Others intimated that the tone of the sport was being lowered, and flotillas would 'encourage the wrong sort'.

If they could not get into the Boat Show, they decided the next best thing would be to advertise to people on their way there. One of the boats was borrowed from Thames Marine (the Snapdragons had been built, but the purchase had not yet been completed). Space was booked at Victoria and Waterloo stations with British Rail advertising. The plan was to show people the boat they could sail in the Greek Islands for their holiday that summer. Of course this location not only caught the eye of travellers to the Show, but of all the commuters struggling to and from work in the gloom of winter weather. A prize draw would be offered to people who wrote their names and addresses and posted them in a box beside the railway station boat, or on the Thames Marine stand at the Show: the prize was a flotilla holiday.

On the appointed day Eric arrived early at Victoria and was waiting by the side entrance to the station. The boat transport was running a little late and he noticed a burly-looking man eyeing him carefully as he loitered there while everyone else was hurrying to and from the trains. After a while the stranger approached him and produced a police warrant card; this was the time when IRA activity was very high. The explanation that he was looking for a boat was not well received, and Eric was invited to go along with policeman, whose stature and facial expression indicated that this was an invitation it would be unwise to decline.

He was led to an office upstairs with a view towards the front of the station, where a senior officer received the report that a suspicious character claimed to be looking for a boat on the railway station. At that moment Eric saw the boat and trailer struggling through the traffic, and interrupted to say, 'It's here now – look out there.' The police saw the funny side, and released their prisoner.

A team of girls distributed leaflets at the station morning and evening, and went to Earls Court during the day to stand outside the Show and hand leaflets to people going in. Of course they were dressed to look smart rather than to keep warm, so they decided to go into the warm of the Show, not realising this would breach the rules of the organisers of the show. Eric explained this to them, but they said everyone was very friendly and they would rather go inside than stay outside in the cold.

Leaflet distribution went very well, and the Thames Marine post-box started to fill very rapidly: more leaflets were printed on the office machine each evening. Not all responses were positive, though: a sailing sage looked through the brochure and surveyed the Snapdragon high and dry opposite Platform 13 at Victoria station and said, 'You'll be on the rocks in three weeks.'

On the last day of the Show the organisers realised that the charming girls did not have a stand and asked them to leave, actually escorting them to the exit. No one minded this because the post-box was full to bursting, the girls had been in the warm and YCA had a hot mailing list.

During the Show Eric spoke to Ray Walsh and his fellow directors of Thames Marine, who were somewhat concerned when they learned that there was not yet a single booking, and they had built eleven boats. Eric tried to reassure them, saying that the size of the mailing list reflected the level of interest in the project.

Straight after the Show the draw took place for the winner of the competition and the mailing list was used to distribute brochures. A few adverts were placed in the yachting press. Shortly afterwards Sally Goodchild in the office took a phone call. She covered the phone with her hand and said, 'There's a chap wants to book!'

By the last week in January the year's flotillas were almost completely full. Of course this was not a huge number of people: at that stage fourteen cruises were planned, the flotilla had ten boats, and in each boat a maximum of four clients. Four further boats were ordered, to be ready later in the season. Eric says this extra order proved to be a mistake, as it briefly created bigger flotillas towards

This advert appeared three times in *Yachts and Yachting* from the late January edition onwards. By the time it was read in the magazine the booking list for the year was virtually full. *YCA*

Sally Goodchild in the office. Maybe this smiling photo was taken as the first orders began to arrive. *Eric Richardson*

the end of the season, which the lead-crews found difficult to handle.

There happened to be a dinghy chandlery within 30 yards of the YCA office in East Grinstead, and a deal was made for the extra equipment needed for the boats. This included fibreglass pram dinghies, as inflatables were very expensive.

The Snapdragons were delivered to Ramsgate, two each week. The plan was to sail them to Calais, then load each pair onto a truck and trailer to be driven to Brindisi. The cross-Channel trip served two purposes: it saved the high cost of transport aboard ferries, and it provided an early shake-down cruise for each boat.

The office was therefore closed at 4.00pm each Friday, and the office staff and a friend or two would go to Ramsgate, step the masts by hand, check and stow the equipment and fit the lifelines. Then, after a meal, they would set off in the middle of the night, depending on tides.

They sailed along the side of the Goodwin Sands on the basis that in the shallow water they would be less likely to encounter shipping, then at a certain point they would run the gauntlet of the Dover Strait and hope that by dawn the lights of Calais would be in sight. They sometimes were: they had no Satnav, of course, though they had RDF, a relatively inexact science.

Crossing the Channel in February was not easy, with fog and other bad weather; at first they did not even have an illuminated compass, but soon a special aircraft-style compass was bought just for the crossings.

On one occasion a pair of boats arrived on the French coast after an uneventful trip, and suddenly the sun came out about 5 miles to the north-east of Calais. Motoring in this fine weather, they started to dismantle the boats, taking off the lifelines, etc. All at once they ran into a bank of fog. They motored in line abreast, just in sight of each other, hoping to find a buoy to give them a positive fix. They were in shallow water so felt safe from shipping until they remembered the hovercraft. 'They have good radar on those things!' Finally they heard the foghorn on a big buoy, which turned out to be the Calais buoy. Once again in a state of euphoria they made their way into the harbour until they had to scatter as a ferry came backwards towards them out of the port.

In Calais they took the boats to pieces again and M Henri at the Calais Yacht Club organised the crane. The drivers saw to the loading and away they went to Brindisi. Then back would come the trucks for the next pair of boats. It turned out that the trailers, designed for short trips once a year, were suffering badly from the long journeys, so M Henri arranged for an excellent welder to make the repairs. In the end there were two trailers, one on the road and one under repair for the next trip.

Once the boats began to be assembled in Brindisi the next issue was the delivery voyage to Greece. In later years there were plenty of people from previous flotillas who were keen to make such a trip, but for the first occasion an advert was placed in the *Sunday Times*. From the applicants

Two Snapdragons at Brindisi in the spring of 1975. The boats ordered for the start of the 1974 season had bilge-keels so they could be sold in the UK if YCA proved unable to take up the order, but these are fin-keeled boats so required modified cradles; otherwise the truck and trailer system was the same. The masts in the photographs belong to boats already afloat! *Eric Richardson.*

Eric selected what seemed to be a suitable team, including Julian Tulloch, an experienced ex-naval man who was put in charge of the operation. They were to be paid for the delivery, including a flight home. Julian later worked for a time as a sea-school skipper at Emsworth, running the YCA three-day courses, and much later started a skippered charter operation in Corfu with his own boat.

They set off, entering Greece at Corfu, but the boats were separated after the Gulf of Corinth. By the time Eric joined them in Greece they were spread all over the Saronic Gulf, some in Spetsai, some in Epidavros, some in Hydra.

The original plan had been to use the harbour at Vouliagmeni, south of Athens and near the airport, which was the location shown in the brochure's chart and in the text describing the route. It became perfectly clear that Vouliagmeni was a place for very big yachts and didn't want to know a group of travel-stained Snapdragons, so it was decided to use Aegina island. This meant that the clients would have a coach transfer to Piraeus, then a short ferry trip.

The boats were finally assembled again at Aegina, and the transfer crews were also assembled. Unfortunately they had got used to the relaxed and happy local life, and the boats, which had now covered a good distance, were not looking too good: the hulls were oily and the cabins looked well lived-in.

It was now late March, and about ten days before the first group of flotillas was due to start. The transfer crews had brought the boats down successfully, but having settled into a lotus-eating mode of life were unlikely to be capable of the necessary burst of energy to clean and prepare them. Eric paid them off, giving them flight tickets for the next day and saying that if they missed the ferry he would not be responsible for them.

Nearby was the Hotel Miranda, a rather basic establishment used by adventurous backpackers, most of them from Australia and New Zealand. Eric went and saw them. He explained the situation and offered pay and food. 'We're up for that!' The

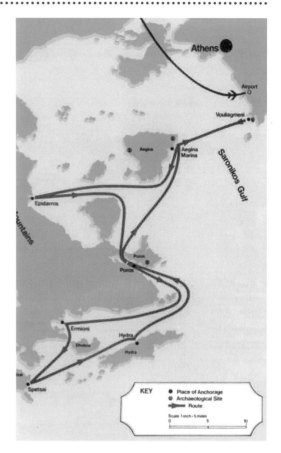

The cruise route as shown in the 1973 brochure. In fact Vouliagmeni was not used, and Aegina became the flotilla base. *YCA*

backpackers went through the boats like a dose of salts, cleaning and scrubbing.

At this stage a serious problem of equipment was discovered. The Snapdragons were equipped with Calor Gas, but in Greece Camping Gas is used, which requires different regulators. YCA was working in Athens with Photis Demas, who had a coach company. He clearly thought the whole project was mad but proved invaluable in solving problems, and helped obtain the eleven new cylinders. However, local regulations did not allow them to be transported on ferries. Eric got round this by buying four suitcases, which proved very heavy to carry.

# 4
# 1974: the first flotilla season

On 10 April 1974 the first flotilla group arrived in Athens. This was a Wednesday, as were all the changeovers that year, a decision taken to avoid congestion. Despite the best efforts of the backpacker team, the boats still needed another six hours' preparation, so Photis proposed taking the group from the airport on a sight-seeing tour of Athens with suitable breaks for refreshment. The clients realised of course that they were the first bunch, and must have set off from home wondering just what they would find when they arrived, so took the honest explanation and the unexpected cultural trip in good part.

The first flotilla hostess was Megan Duncan, an Australian who had originally been the au pair to Eric's newly born daughter and was caught up in the whole enterprise. She was a hugely capable person and ideal for the hostess role.

At about 6.30pm, just as the light was starting to fade, the ferry arrived at Aegina. Megan led the crew, smart in YCA tee-shirts and shorts, down to meet them. The Snappies were on the Aegina quay looking pristine, with suitable music on their cassette players, the cabin lights on, and the starter packs of food on board. The clients were taken to their boats, and Megan suggested they settle in, then meet at the taverna across the road where tables had been booked. Flotilla holidays had begun.

The next day the first skippers' briefing was held. The plan was to start with an easy trip, so they were taken to Aghia Marina. This was nothing to do

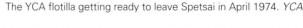

The YCA flotilla getting ready to leave Spetsai in April 1974. *YCA*

with places with lazy-lines or shore power, but a bay not far from Aegina town, named after the church of Aghia Marina and offering a visit to a temple. It is now a centre of tourism on the island, but was formerly full of olive trees and vines.

Here they were to anchor off, and go ashore in dinghies to one of the tavernas. There was a gentle sail round, but what they hadn't realised was that this was one of the few surfing beaches in Greece.

The boats were anchored successfully, but as the crews went ashore in the little pram dinghies they got very wet: the waves were small, but the cockleshells would be turned sideways by them and then the next wave would come aboard. The water was very shallow so no one came to any harm, even those whose boats capsized altogether.

Epidavros was the next destination. Unusually there was fog on the way, and the lead-crew started to suggest radar as standard equipment. The flotilla found the narrow harbour entrance and moored in the shallow water, discovering the idyllic location and able to visit the wonderful amphitheatre built out of the hillside.

Many of the routines and arrangements that are still familiar were quickly established. The lead-boat was at first called the pilot-boat, and piloted the flotilla more closely than is now the case, using a system of flags to give instructions, though its crew, as is usual now, consisted of a skipper, an engineer and a hostess.

The daily briefing was called the skippers' meeting, and advice about places to eat in the evening was offered as well as course instructions and a weather report. Barbecues were an early feature simply because of a lack of places to eat in some of the villages.

The flotilla then continued via Spetsai and Poros. By the time it returned to Gatwick, Eric was back in England. He met the participants at the airport and was delighted by their very positive reactions to their holiday.

As the succeeding flotillas continued during May and June, a mystery mechanical problem arose: the alternators on the Yanmar engines began to fail. Replacements were airfreighted out at high cost, but the reason for the failures was unclear. Thames Marine suggested that the crews were filling the cockpits with water to take a bath, but everyone denied it. Eventually John Scott from the

Joan Gould, an American writer, took part in several early YCA flotillas, and in an article published in the *New York Times* she said this of flotilla skippers: 'Tony, our British sailing master, is blond, tanned, tousled, competent – a Viking lad who's been blown off course. All sailing masters are blond, tanned, tousled, competent.'

Her admiration for Tony and her description of him is something that other male skippers would no doubt be happy with, but the very first skipper was actually a woman. Janet Green was skipper of this flotilla, Megan Duncan was the hostess and David Archer was the engineer. Subsequent female skippers will be glad to know that things started this way.

The theatre at Epidavros. *G. Zygmund*

supplier flew out and applied his considerable engineering skills to the issue. The problem turned out to be threefold.

A little water was seeping in through the stern gland and this built up if the bilges were not pumped regularly. The prop shaft ran in a gully in the hull of the boat and the rotating shaft flicked water into the air: not enough to wet anything visibly but enough, in the hot Greek weather, to create a salt-water saturated atmosphere in the compartment, which shorted the diodes on the alternators. Thames Marine modified the moulding very slightly and there was no further trouble.

In this first season YCA knew the eyes of the sailing establishment were upon it. Opinions in yacht club bars and the more staid sections of the yachting press ranged from scorn that anyone should need to sail in a group to the certainty that there would soon be regrettable maritime disasters.

For the first few years flotilla sailors were seldom let off the lead in the way that is common today. This was from caution as everyone, including the lead-crews, gained experience in managing the fleets, but also because there were few other yachts around in

*Left* A Snappie settling into a new home in 1974. Note the GRP dinghy – inflatables were too expensive. *YCA*

*Below* The waterfront at Poros in 1974. *YCA*

those days to lend a hand in the case of a gear failure while one of the boats was isolated. Boats equipped with VHF radios were some way in the future.

## War

The outbreak of war between Greece and Turkey before the first flotilla season was halfway through must have put any other difficulties in the shade. An item in *The Times* in early July referred to a different sort of shipping:

**'Flare-up in Cyprus may disrupt shipping**
Turmoil has overtaken the extremely influential Greek shipping community and the freight markets as a result of the Turkish landings in Cyprus, with the tramp shipping trades in danger of total disruption.

Mobilisation of the Greek armed forces is already a factor – Greek-crewed vessels could lose men to the army, either from being reservists or from patriotic fervour. This could be happening according to reports.

At the moment though the biggest headache in the market is the possibility of declared war between Greece and Turkey, which could allow charter paths involving Greek flag or Greek-controlled ships to be cancelled.'

The newspaper item went on to discuss possible rises in costs in the 'dry cargo market' as well as for oil tankers. At this stage coverage in the British press was about the possible effect on international trade rather than on everyday life in the countries involved, and certainly not about YCA's early steps in the tourism industry.

On 15 July the Greek military government ('The Colonels', who were becoming increasingly unpopular) backed a coup in Cyprus, in an attempt to unite the island with Greece.

On 17 July a flotilla flight left from Gatwick with no problems. Janet Green telephoned saying, 'The locals think there will be a war!'

On the 20th Turkey invaded Cyprus. Athens airport was shut and for a while it became impossible to get into or out of Greece. On the 23rd the Colonels' government fell, and democracy returned to Greece. On the 24th this *Times* headline signalled a return to peace:

**'Mr. Karamanlis returns to Greece to head national unity government**
The chiefs of the Greek armed forces, shaken by events in Cyprus, yesterday called on professional politicians to form a government of national unity. The new Government will be headed by Mr. Constantine Karamanlis, the former Prime Minister, who early today flew back to Athens from exile in Paris in an aircraft supplied by the French government…
In Cyprus the ceasefire appeared to be taking hold.'

On 30 July a peace deal was agreed, which partitioned Cyprus, and the following day the flotilla flight left without incident. This was very lucky because any stoppage would have broken YCA financially at that time – Eric can remember being very concerned. The British Foreign Office never advised against travelling, though, and the Greeks were very loath to harm their tourist industry in mid-season.

Janet reported that the tavernas had no waiters because they had all been called up. However, by mid-August things were back to normal as the young men slowly filtered home and everything opened up again.

# 5
# 1975

At the end of the first season another eleven Snapdragons were ordered: all at once Ray Walsh's confidence was repaid. After the first batch of boats, the orders were for the fin-keel version, which for 1975 would provide two fleets in the Saronic Gulf, each of twelve boats plus the lead-boat.

The existing boats were kept at Epidavros over the winter and anti-fouled there. Compared with later years this was a rather unsophisticated lay-up period: one feature was that a local Greek whom they knew said that his father-in-law would really love to varnish the wooden rubbing-strips on the Snappies. He did a very thorough job with a six-inch brush, which considerably modified the appearance of the boats.

During the winter new lead-crews were appointed. Janet Green had left, though David Brooke-Smith, who was one of the new skippers, remembers Janet and her boyfriend visiting during

the season to say hello. David had been working in the Caribbean on board the *America*, a beautiful replica of the schooner that won the race leading to the America's Cup series. He was interviewed in Crawley, and joined the new staff in late February to travel to Greece.

The staff transport turned out to be an elderly Land Rover in which the seven of them drove to Greece, towing a trailer with two masts and some other spares. David believes their top speed was 45mph when going down an alp. Also jammed into the Land Rover were Rosie Hayden, who became Mrs Brooke-Smith, and Charlie Head, who was the engineer in their flotilla and is still fitting out boats back in his native Australia. David Archer, the engineer from the first season, was in the group and was a sort of elder statesman, since he was the only person in the company (or anywhere in the world) with practical experience of managing a flotilla.

David Archer, the engineer for the first flotilla in 1974 who became in the 1975 season the world's leading expert on flotillas. *YCA*

*I*n the January 1975 edition of *Power and Sail* magazine a detailed article was printed, with many coloured views of the sailing area. It began:

'No matter at what point you gain an interest in sailing, or at whatever age, there is inevitably a time when you say to yourself, "Oh, wouldn't it be fabulous to sail for a couple of weeks in the warmth of the Mediterranean?" This part of the globe seems to be reserved for the wealthy Continentals and the even wealthier British yachtsmen. Well, for a comparatively low cost it can be a reality now. A little over a year ago a new company calling itself Yacht Cruising Associates took the wise decision to buy and sail a fleet of sailboats to the Aegean and make holidaymaking in Greece a reality for many enthusiastic yachtsmen.'

The subsequent description of the flotilla experience would be thoroughly recognisable to any flotilla sailor since then, though maybe there was more emphasis on cultural sight-seeing on the mainland. The first impressions and the highlights are much the same, though: the varied sailing experience of the other crews, the starter-packs on the boats, the Greek food at the tavernas, the skipper (it must have been Janet Green, though she only stayed with YCA for a year), 'with the patience of a saint'. There is typically British sympathy for the octopus killed and tenderised on the concrete quay, and reference to good memories to last 'through the winter'.

Snappy snapshots: impressions of flotilla sailing. *YCA*

Skipper David Brooke-Smith and hostess Rosie Hayden. *David Brooke-Smith*

Once in Greece they set to to prepare the original fourteen bilge-keel Snapdragons for the new season. They would sail a group of boats to the next bay, where the sand was quite firm and sloped gently, put one of them onto the trailer and haul it out with the Land Rover. The boat would be scrubbed and anti-fouled, but getting it back into the water was more difficult; sometimes it took four boats harnessed together to pull another back down the beach and float it off the trailer.

The new Snapdragons arrived at the last moment, but there was also a change of personnel as two of the party, originally designated as skipper and hostess of the second flotilla, left. This was lucky for David Brooke-Smith, who was expecting to work with the older boats but now took on the new boats and the first group of clients.

The plan had been for David Archer to take both new skippers round the islands to familiarise them with the harbours, but of course there was no time. The day that the clients were expected, the boats were still being prepared; however, a

three-hour delay because of snow at Gatwick, although dreadful for the travellers, allowed just enough time for everyone to clean up ready to receive them. 'Good evening!' said David as they arrived on the quay in darkness. 'Nope!' said a Canadian client, who had had about enough by then.

There was another group of engineers at Epidavros, sent out to do some last-minute GRP work on the boats, and the Canadian was even less amused the next morning when his party was turned off their boat for structural work. Within three days the magic of the flotilla lifestyle had relaxed him, and he was enjoying his holiday. A constant theme when talking to the lead-crews from those days is the way the clients relaxed into the experience. David says:

'We'd get stressed executives and their families, people whose life was all Now! Now! Now! After a few days they'd settle into life at flotilla speed.'

A modern skipper would say the same thing, but in the early days the clients too were pioneering. Take the sense of achievement of a family, this year or next, when they first moor their flotilla boat successfully, and multiply it a good many times to imagine how it was in the mid-1970s when there would be no yachts in the harbour except for the flotilla, and none to be seen out at sea either.

David says he was a very anxious skipper, who kept the boats in his flotilla firmly under control.

'I was terrified about the clients, who seemed to have no skills. I came from a background of professional crews. My meeting on the first day lasted for an hour, though I broke it up into three sections and dropped in a reference to something like sharks every now and then to wake them up.

At first I used to order them to follow me on the water very closely, and would dash about in *Merlin* telling any stragglers to catch up. In that respect I was quite different from Mike Cox, who used to cruise along in a relaxed way in the middle of his flotilla.'

Already the tradition had been established of calling all YCA lead-boats *Merlin*.

Mike Cox had arrived as a skipper just as David's first group set sail, and took charge of the older Snapdragons. For this season David Archer was his engineer and Susan Woolrych the sailing hostess. Previously he had been organising, and taking part in, adventure and survival training courses for military personnel while with Joint Services. Initially based at Hamble, he moved to the British Keil Yacht Club on the Baltic where he skippered a 50-foot yacht sailing three-week cruises. The crew were always a mixture of army and air force personnel, both men and officers, and his brief was to give them some sea experience and generally, as the Services would say, a character-building experience! The successful finale to each cruise was bringing the 50-footer under sail, bows to the quay with her stern secured to two piles. The moorings at Keil were immediately below the OC's office window. (Maybe we should remember this to put into perspective our own experiences in mooring stern-to in a side-wind at Fiscardo under the eyes of late-lunching tourists.)

This photo of Mike Cox was taken in 1982. *YCA*

At the end of Mike's career with HM Services he was chosen as one of the two heavy-weather helmsmen aboard *British Soldier* in the 1973 Whitbread Round the World Race. In the southern ocean during the night there would be just two men on deck: the helmsman, harnessed to the wheel facing forward, and the helmsman's friend, facing aft. The latter's job was to watch the waves as they approached the stern and tell the helmsman when to take a breath before being momentarily engulfed by the seas breaking into the cockpit.

The move to Epidavros meant that clients could be brought to the boats on a land route, although the journey took about three hours. The bay was sheltered in most conditions, and the fishermen were happy for the flotilla boats to be sharing the quay with them. Once a season there would be a big easterly wind, though.

One changeover weekend the boats were being prepared in the usual dead calm. A slight breeze sprang up, and within three minutes it had turned into a full force eight, blowing straight onto the harbour wall. With their anchors dragging, the boats had to be taken one by one out into the bay and anchored safely, then their preparation done out there. It was still blowing when the coaches arrived from the airport in the evening and the clients were ferried out to their boats in *Merlin*. By the morning conditions were back to normal.

# Flotilla Yacht Cruising

Flotilla yacht cruising is a new sailing holiday idea that was first conceived by Yacht Cruising Associates in 1972. After a year of detailed planning, the idea was made known to the British sailing fraternity during 1973 and was received with considerable enthusiasm. Over 700 people took advantage of these holidays last year and as this brochure goes to press we have already been asked to reserve over 20% of the total yachts available for people who wish to rebook their holidays in 1975.

Many people would love to charter a small yacht and sail the Greek Islands with their family or friends. Unfortunately there have always been two major problems—the high cost of chartering a suitable yacht when added to the normal air fare and how confident the skipper feels about sailing off into the blue at the helm of a completely strange boat. The flotilla cruise concept solves both these problems. The high cost of air travel is dramatically reduced because we are able to guarantee British Airways a set number of passengers throughout the sailing season. The cost of running our yachts is the same as for normal "bareboat" chartering, except that we tend to obtain greater utilization and hence our costs are spread over a larger number of people.

Whilst sailing from island to island, we cruise in company and this means that we are able to accept relatively inexperienced skippers. Only one member of your crew needs to have sailing experience and providing they are really competent dinghy sailors, that will be sufficient. The flotilla is accompanied by a pilot yacht with our staff aboard who have knowledge of the local area and weather conditions.

YCA have spent months planning your cruise route so that each new port of call is a highlight and you sail through some of the most beautiful and safe waters in the Mediterranean. Our staff know the cruising area thoroughly and can tell you the best places for snorkelling or a beach barbeque. They will advise you about excursions ashore to historical sites and other places of interest and will also be ready to help organize the practical necessities that go towards making a cruise successful. Where to obtain fresh water, ice and other stores or where you can moor without upsetting the local fishermen! These things are very important when cruising and often terribly difficult to find out yourself especially when you don't speak the language. YCA are on very good terms with the local Greek people and when you fly our burgee at your masthead you are assured of a warm and friendly welcome in the Islands. All the yachts in the flotilla are identical and this means that we are able to carry aboard our pilot yacht a very comprehensive spares holding. One member of our sailing staff is an experienced marine mechanic and we also have our own shore facilities for sail and rigging repairs.

Our flotillas normally consist of 12 yachts. You sail as a flotilla only whilst travelling between anchorages and the average flotilla sail is about 4 to 5 hours. This allows for a very leisurely itinerary and once at your anchorage your yacht is entirely your own to use for independent exploring and sailing. You will find that our sailing staff, although ready to help and give advice when requested, are equally pleased to leave you to your own devices to enjoy your holiday as you wish. Sailing people are independent people and these cruises have been designed around that very important fact.

For 1975 we have altered the cruise route so that you have four consecutive days at the most southerly point for independent sailing. You may decide to use the old port at Spetsai as your base and day sail to the many interesting coves around the island and beside the adjacent mainland coast. Should you have more ambitious sailing plans, you are free to explore the Argolis Gulf which reaches as far north as ancient Navplion.

For people who are thinking of buying their own cruising yachts there can be no better way of introducing the family to cruising. From April through to October the Greek Islands are a sailing paradise and the flotilla yacht cruising concept now enables many more people to enjoy this type of holiday in comfort and safety.

---

After one year's experience and experimentation, this publicity document from YCA sets out with more confidence what a flotilla cruise offers. Interestingly the flotillas are already being described as a step in extending sailing experience.

To this day Barrie Neilson of Sailing Holidays makes this point, saying that in the last quarter of the twentieth century the major sail-training revolution in the UK was that folk could build up their skills, with their family coming along and being involved too, in warm and safe conditions, rather than associating sailing with flogging around the British coast in oilskins.

'We've made people realise they can do it. No need to get frozen in the Channel, no need to spend a fortune just mooring a boat in the UK.'

And Ellen MacArthur has said that 'Flotillas are the modern way to learn to sail: they've introduced more women to sailing in thirty years than anything else ever.' *YCA*

*Barrie Neilson*

*Above* A deserted cove south of Korfos. During 1975 Epidavros was used as the base for changeovers and the route shown in the brochure extended right round the peninsula from Korfos in the north-east to harbours of the Gulf of Argolis in the west, and was used for independent exploring. *YCA*

*Below* The revised route for the second year in the Saronic Gulf. *YCA*

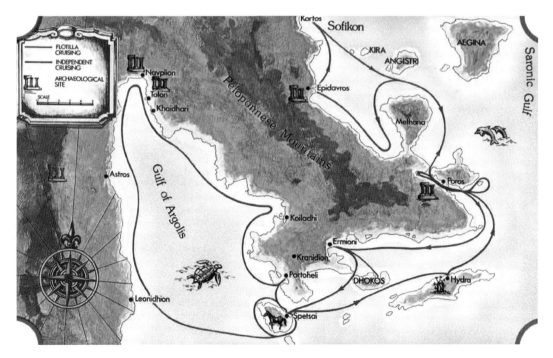

```
Yacht Diesel Engine

    Controls

The throttle and gear lever are situa
of the cockpit well.  Small lever is
forward to increase power.  Large le\
ahead. upright for neutral and full l
you will see the starter key, oil anc
light and decompressor knob.
Nearby you will see the engine key, oil and charge circuit
warning light.  The decompressor knob is inside the starboard
cockpit locker.


    Starting.

1.    Gear lever in neutral.

2.    Throttle full forward.

3.  Turn engine key to first position and check that oil and
charging lights are on.

4.    Pull decompresser knob and turn starter key to second position
      as you would to start your car.  Hold for 2/3 seconds - engine
      makes high pitched whine - release decompresser knob and engine
      will start.   IMPORTANT  make sure key switch returns to
      first position - this is very important because if key jams in
      starting position the starter motor will remain in gear with
      the motor and will burn itself out.  If your key switch has a
      tendency to stick tell our sailing staff.

5.    Throttle back slowly until you reach tick over and leave engine
      running for a few minutes to warm up.

6.    Check that charge light and oil light switch themselves off.

7.    Look over the stern and check that engine cooling water is
      coming out of the exhaust - if not stop engine and tell our
      sailing staff.

    Stopping.

1.    Gear lever in neutral.

2.    Close throttle - engine will stop.

3   Turn off engine key*  Please see warning below.

4.    DO NOT turn off fuel.

    *   Do not for any reason turn the starter key to the
        "off" position whilst the engine is running.  This
        will burn out the alternator and could ruin your holiday.
        THIS IS VERY IMPORTANT.
```

Instructions from the YCA 1975 notes on starting the engine. *YCA*

For the 1975 season a 34-page A4 booklet called *Flotilla Cruising Notes* was produced. This dealt with everything from arrival at Athens and children's safety to management of the boat including the marine toilets (no holding tanks, so only to be used at sea), a system of using flags to receive communication from the pilot-boat (*Merlin 1* or *Merlin 2*) and very detailed hand-drawn harbour plans. There were full pages on starting the engine using the electric starter and decompressor knob, and on starting the engine by hand.

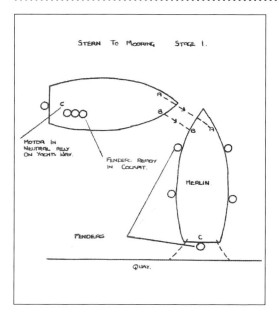

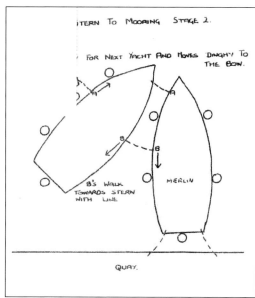

Drawings from the YCA 1975 *Flotilla Cruising Notes* showing stages in the mooring process. Interestingly, the process described is not the bows-to method of dropping the kedge over the stern, which became standard later. It is stern-to, but certainly not the method that has become the most common recently with the advent of bigger boats that go astern reliably and have electric windlasses. The pilot yacht would moor first, and the next boat would aim to drop gently alongside before taking out the bow anchor using the dinghy. *YCA*

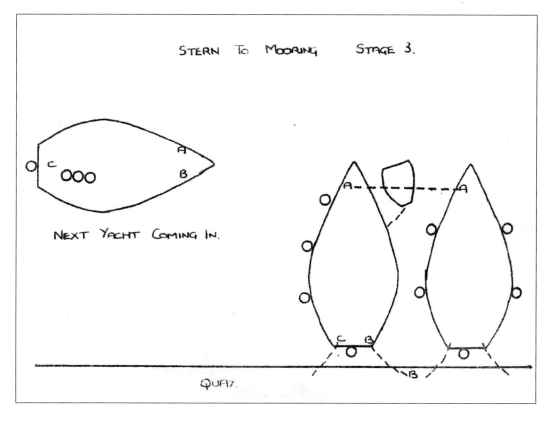

# The 'Holiday' programme

Eric had been talking to the BBC about featuring flotillas on its *Holiday* programme. Finally agreement was reached to make a film during 1975, to be shown in early 1976.

A Carter 33 was chartered as a film boat, and the BBC team joined the flotilla at Spetsai. The YCA personnel, well used to reacting to events, making things happen and organising their day's work according to the weather and the needs of twelve groups of sailors, were struck by the kid-gloves treatment accorded to the film crew. It quickly became evident that they needed good food regularly and plenty of breaks.

As the boats left the harbour, with the lifejacketed film crew looking less than comfortable, it became clear that the Carter would not motor as fast as the Snapdragons. Surreptitious messages were passed: 'Divert!' 'Slow down!' But the film was made.

Now the planning for the next season depended on knowing how the film would be received, as well as when it would be shown. In those days tour operators would begin booking immediately after Christmas, and hope to get the bulk of their bookings by mid-February. There had been an unofficial promise that the flotilla film would be shown early in the year, but the BBC was of course not prepared to guarantee anything. (When *Holiday* began in 1969, special permission had been required from the Governors to mention particular brands and prices.)

Eric rang the programme office later in the year to ask how the film had turned out. 'I think it will be fine.' He explained that this would be major publicity for YCA, and that he was considering doubling his fleets for the next year. 'Oh, I couldn't possibly advise you to do anything like that!' Finally, 'All I can say is that it will be a good film. I don't think you will be disappointed.'

On the basis of this nod or wink, twenty-four boats were ordered from Thames Marine. This time they were larger boats: Mirage 28s. One fleet of the new boats went to the Saronic Gulf, and one to the Sporades.

Finally the film came out, and the season was sold out straightaway. In hindsight Eric says that he should have borrowed more at this point to build more boats, though Thames Marine would not have been able to provide more. For now YCA was no longer the only game in town.

After the initial *Holiday* programme filming, the BBC returned several more times. Here a crew is filming a suitably glamorous couple who are being taught to sail: actors Patrick Mower and Suzanne Danielle. Strict regulation of scuba diving to preserve antiquities meant that the Greek authorities needed to keep a close eye on the underwater filming. The two policemen who accompanied the film-boat dozed off after the third hour of setting-up the equipment, but some good shots of anchors reaching the bottom of the bay and of Suzanne swooping lithely under the boat's keel were captured for transmission. *YCA*

# 6
# 1976: new companies, new areas

*F*or the 1976 season YCA offered 'share a yacht' listings for clients or couples not wanting to take on a yacht by themselves, and three-day sea-school courses in a Snapdragon based at Chatham and a Macwester (Eric's own boat, earning its keep) operating from Emsworth.

In addition, a new route in the Sporades had been prepared:

'The Sporades Islands are more exposed to the north than the Saronic Islands and we can promise you some exciting sailing. We will have two flotillas in each area: there will be a flotilla of Snapdragon 747s in the Saronic and Sporades islands and in addition each area will have a slightly smaller flotilla of our new 6 berth Mirage 28.'

Orei on Evvia island was used as the flotilla base.

Once again the new YCA staff met at Crawley, but this year they were flown to Greece rather than dispatched in the Land Rover. Amongst them were

Snapdragons moored at Balza creek in May 1976. *YCA*

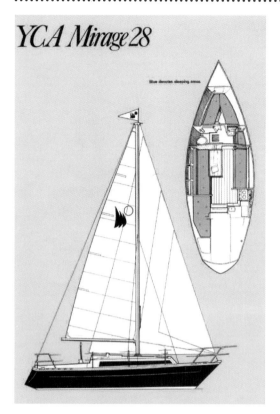

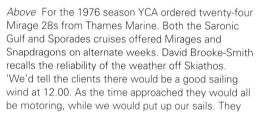

*YCA Mirage 28*

*Above* For the 1976 season YCA ordered twenty-four Mirage 28s from Thames Marine. Both the Saronic Gulf and Sporades cruises offered Mirages and Snapdragons on alternate weeks. David Brooke-Smith recalls the reliability of the weather off Skiathos. 'We'd tell the clients there would be a good sailing wind at 12.00. As the time approached they would all be motoring, while we would put up our sails. They

assumed we had very special powers when the wind filled in and the pilot-boat sailed past them as they struggled to get their sails hoisted.' *YCA*

*Above* The cover of the 1977 YCA brochure. Eric Richardson had himself hoisted up the mast with his camera to take this photo of hostess Angie Keys (later Angie Blackman). *Eric Richardson*

Nigel Blackman and Angie Keys, another couple who married after working together as flotilla leaders. They were to be David Brook-Smith's crew on the Mirage flotilla on the new route. The plan was for David and Nigel to work their way round the route, surveying harbours and preparing advice for the clients. Unfortunately the boat had an engine problem, so the survey was never completed, and for a good deal of the first fortnight they were going in blind. Angie's immediate role was to 'sort out' the tavernas, and in some of the villages she had to go ashore in a dinghy, rush round to get an idea of where it was possible to eat, then go round the boats as they moored, passing on her advice.

However, in some cases it was possible to plan ahead a little. All three of the crew recounted the

story of the tiny harbour of Pigardi where, as time went on, it was evident that the weekly arrival of the boats was making a real difference to the wealth of the isolated community. They wanted to take the flotilla there as it would make a good short journey before setting off towards Skiathos. There was only one very small taverna, and when the owner was told that a group of boats with several people on board would like to call he was quite sceptical – he'd heard stories like that before. On the first week three boatloads of people turned up, which caused a commotion in the kitchen – the total tourism of the previous year had just been exceeded. Ten boats arriving on the second week brought about the sudden and unexpected demise of a number of chickens.

Skiathos harbour. *YCA*

Not every taverna felt it had a fair share of the custom, though. David had been advised that a particular taverna in Poros was worth going to. In fact, it seemed a bit cold and boring, but they persevered with it even though a new one had opened nearby that seemed much more friendly and interesting, with music and some dancing. When they finally began to visit the newer taverna the owner of the original one took umbrage, and wrote to Eric in London to accuse David of asking for a kick-back to ensure his custom. Eric wrote in reply saying that he didn't believe a word of it. To have trust demonstrated in this way was hugely important and David relates this story as an example of the style of Eric's leadership. Angie says that Eric always asked you what you thought and gave the impression of listening – rare qualities amongst the others she has worked for. The early pilot-boat crews were all operating a long way from wherever their head office was. It was very hard work indeed, with no days off over a nine-month period and every problem having to be sorted out on the spot by themselves.

The distance from any supervision led to incidents that would nowadays lead to considerable filling-in of Health and Safety Report forms. David remembers the drunken client who rolled off the harbour wall at Spetsai into safe shallow water covering sand amidst hundreds of yards of sharp rocks. On another occasion he was walking back to the boats when all at once there was a big explosion. Images of leaking gas-bottles and burning boats flashed though his mind, then a tree-stump flew over the wall; a farmer was clearing his land with the help of black powder.

Perhaps the most unexpected memory from David is that skippers were much better paid in those days. He drew about £15 a week from his salary, and at the end of the season remembers going back to the UK and using his end-of-season bonus and savings to buy a Rolex and a complete new outfit of clothes.

David's father and mother helped with the winter work that year at Korfos. This was not the comfortable alternative to an English spring that it might have seemed; they were living aboard one of the boats, all of which were moored in the bay, when they were pushed ashore despite having two anchors out and the engine at full chat. They knew their way around boats, having met on a topsail schooner before the war, and David is proud of the unusual boast that he is one of four generations of his family to make a living under sail.

The 1975 and 1976 YCA brochures contained a page offering independent cruising on 33-foot yachts in the Cyclades through an associate company. No bookings were received for these 'bare-boat' holidays. They were a little more expensive than the flotilla boats: the high-season price per person in 1976 for four people on a Snapdragon was £168, and for a Mirage 28 it was £196, while these Carter 33s were offered at £243. In addition, it was emphasised that they were only suitable for more experienced sailors. The ease with which the bookings were filled for the flotillas continued to show that the original decision to provide 'cruising in company' was the right one.

However, two new companies were offering flotilla holidays during that season. One of them lasted only a few years as a separate operation, though the use of bigger boats was an early sign of things to come rather later. The other specialised in Ionian flotillas and continues to do so to this day.

## MCS in the Sporades

Eric says:

'We had prepared our new route in the Sporades and at the Boat Show were surprised to find a competitor, Mediterranean Charter Services. They were planning to operate on "our" new route. They reckoned they were an up-market version and were using Maxi 95s with a motor yacht as a lead-boat and offering an owner leaseback system. The Maxis had a separate aft cabin and centre cockpit and were good boats. However, they were really designed for Northern Europe and in the Med the aft cabins were very hot. Our lead-crews were envious of the motor yacht.'

## FSC in the Ionian

The other new company was called Greek Island Yachting Holidays, though the name soon changed to Flotilla Sailing Club. It is the only one of the pioneering companies to maintain its independence to this day, changing its name again in 1990 to Sailing Holidays.

Tom Keen, a British businessman, had attempted to charter a yacht on a YCA flotilla. Having a background of derring-do in the RAF in the Far East during the war and of imaginatively creating his own businesses since then, he was concerned about his two sons Thomas and David, who were, as he saw it, 'wasting their lives' down in Corfu. When they said, 'We don't care what it is Dad, so long as it's on a yacht and it's down here in Greece,' he got a yachting magazine and when he phoned YCA was told they were all booked up. He realised that here was a concept that made good business sense.

Tom put down the phone and looked for yacht manufacturers. Like Eric two years earlier he found little immediate interest, but finally spoke to Des Pollard who was building 27-foot Jaguars at the old airfield at Southend. Jaguars were basically a copy of Catalinas from the USA, and, unlike most British boats, were designed for warm weather. When Tom said he wanted to buy twenty-four boats Des nearly fell off his chair. It wasn't possible to build that many in time, but initially Tom bought about fifteen, then between them they found seven or eight second-hand ones. He phoned his boys and said that there would be some trucks with boats arriving at Ancona.

During the 1976 season GIYH got started with one flotilla in the Corfu area. The choice of the Ionian was an inspired one with far-reaching results, but of course it arose from the fact that Tom's sons were living there at the time. Martin and Sue Evans, a brother and sister team who had sailed down from Suffolk to Greece in a converted lifeboat, were the first GIYH skipper and hostess.

In this third season the concept of flotilla sailing had become established and this year there were more than 5,000 people exploring the Greek Islands. Cruising sailors were going flotilla sailing and the established sailing fraternity had realised that these holidays offered good, safe, enjoyable

*Above* Jaguars at Lakka Town Quay: even in 1980 not another boat is in sight and the quay is a sort of wharf area. *Sailing Holidays*

*Below* Tom Keen (right) is obviously thoroughly enjoying the Boat Show. The model is equipped for protection against the sun, against thirst and against drowning, but looks a little unsure whether she's protected against musicians. *Sailing Holidays*

*Left* Sailing Holidays celebrated twenty years in the Ionian by publishing this collage in their 1996 brochure. *Barrie Neilson*

*Right* Sayiadha before the harbour was built. *Sailing Holidays*

*Right* Hauling out: pictures like this were taken each year to prove that the boats had been anti-fouled. The scaffolding framework was designed and built in England and taken to Sivota, where it could still be seen until recently. *Mike Cox*

sailing at an unbeatable price. At the end of the year YCA ordered 42,000 information leaflets and 22,000 cruising brochures.

During the remainder of the 1970s and '80s a series of small companies were established to take advantage of what seemed to be an attractive business pattern. There were tax advantages for British companies buying yachts as their capital equipment, and it was clear that a strong customer base existed for the flotillas. These small companies soon discovered that the business was not as simple as it seemed, and many lasted only a short time, while others, during the 1990s or later, combined or were swallowed by multinational travel companies as the flotilla holiday entered the mainstream of the industry.

# 7
# Growth in the late 1970s

## 1977

Rod Heikell, later known throughout the cruising world for his pilot books and guides, turned up at Corfu having brought his own tiny boat down from the UK. He helped out with some Jaguar 22s for FSC as well as with cleaning and repair work on turn-around days.

The 22-footers were boats that Tom Keen had bought to encourage couples to try sailing, as the 27s were considered four-to-six-person yachts at that time. They were 'pop tops' with an outboard motor in a well, and these little engines made it difficult for them to keep up with the bigger boats when motoring.

In 1977 YCA moved a flotilla of Snapdragons and one of Mirages to the Ionian. Once again, by the end of the Boat Show berths were sold out completely, and this pattern of selling out by the end of the Show was maintained until nearly the end of the 1970s.

Mike Cox returned to the UK to work in the YCA office. The company was offering Mirages in the Sporades starting at Orei, Snapdragons and Mirages in the Saronic Gulf starting at Korfos, and Snapdragons and Mirages in the Ionian.

Angie and Nigel Blackman had spent part of the summer crewing on a privately owned 71-footer but had found it less enjoyable than their flotilla year. They took the opportunity to do some work for YCA in the Ionian, and while at Nidri Angie had an experience that was rare then and rarer still at any later time: she was invited onto Aristotle Onassis's island, Scorpios, and visited his yacht *Christina*. The invitation was of course not from the great man himself, but from a group of his security men, whom she met over a drink in a bar.

All the same, when Angie says that with YCA they had been given times in their life that they will never forget she means working on the flotillas, and all the early lead-crews, from whichever company, describe their time with the yachts in a similar way.

## More companies in 1978

For the 1978 season Rod Heikell was 'poached' by another new company, Crawford Perry Travel. John Kaye and his partner Richard Perry ran a skiing operation and had decided to start up a summer sailing programme, CPT Cruising in Greece. (This company later became CPT Sailing in Greece, then Falcon Sailing, then Sovereign, then Sun World, and currently Neilson.)

John Charnley, who had a small 'bare-boat' company with Sabre 27s, had found the Cobra 850, built at Waterlooville where John Lockwood could turn them out at a good price. The Cobras were designed by David Feltham, who also designed the Mirages, which were used by YCA and others.

The initial order was for nine Cobras for CPT and three for John Charnley's Greeksail, based in Poros. They were all trucked down to Brindisi and from there sailed across to Greece and the Saronic. By the end of 1978 CPT was running nearly twenty boats.

In 1978 Tom Keen was expanding FSC. One of the Jaguar flotillas was based at Levkas in this year, and was successful despite the six-hour transfer from Corfu by coach, ferry, coach and finally the ferry across the Levkas Canal. Customers appreciated that it was a proper Greek place. Other

*Above* Mourtos in 1979. *Sailing Holidays*

*Right* A fleet of Jaguars at Kassiope, Corfu. *Sailing Holidays*

companies had been concerned about the sewage arrangements at Levkas, but the water was fine – it was the mud banks of the canal that smelled!

Tom could see that there was a great demand for this type of holiday as he was in direct contact with people on the phone, and his problem was getting enough boats to cope with demand. His son Thomas, who had taken the lead in running the business in Greece, realised that people would be looking for boats that were a bit more sleek and lively, so he got Tom to buy six UFO 27s, a boat designed as a cruiser-racer. Four of them were to be fitted out in Corfu, so only hulls were sent out.

These faster boats brought the total with FSC to nearly fifty boats, mostly Jaguars but also a dozen Westerly Pembrokes (the fin-keel version of the Centaur), which he had taken over from a short-lived Greek company. But in this year a tragedy hit: Thomas was drowned while moving a boat single-handed after a breakdown at Paxos. Tom was shattered, as were the rest of the team on the spot.

The UFOs were used as lead-boats for a few years before essentially being abandoned until, much later, Barrie Neilson found a couple of them in a field beside a boat yard and decided to restore one because of their history. This is *Pocket Rocket*, well known to those who race in the Ionian Regattas.

The YCA *Cruising Notes* were revised in 1978, but still give fascinating details of life on board: there are instructions for using the marine toilet, but only on the Mirages, and since there were no holding tanks yet these could only be used at sea.

'When everyone is ready *Merlin* will sail to the front of the flotilla and set course… Please do not go ahead of *Merlin* or fall so far back that you cannot read her sail number – if you start to fall back use your motor to catch up. *Merlin* will wait for people to catch up by heaving to, but it is rather trying for other members of the flotilla to be kept waiting.'

(Despite these instructions the brochure mentions more days of independent sailing in each of the areas.)

YCA was offering flotillas in three regions. The Saronic route was modified to allow more time at Spetsai; alternate flotillas started at Korfos and Navolion to allow a more leisurely journey. The Mirage 26 is mentioned in the brochure as well as the established 28 (YCA now had twenty-nine of these), and there is a note saying that the prototype of a YCA-commissioned yacht would be sailing in the Ionian this year, the first reference to the YCA 29. The note went on to say: 'YCA now employs 23 staff, and is responsible for 66 yachts'. There is an estimate that 3,200 people would sail on YCA flotillas in the coming year. Also, a French version of the YCA brochure was printed in this year.

Transport of the boats was still not simple. In the mid-1970s there was a French transport strike and a group of Snapdragons sailed through a trawler blockade at Calais. Realising there would be difficulties, Eric took (another!) pretty au pair girl, Chantal, with him to charm the Customs and to interpret. Unfortunately, once with her fellow

Anchored at Meganisi in 1979.
*J. Yeld*

The waterfront at Hydra in June 1978. *YCA*

countrymen Chantal immediately changed sides and was more hindrance then help. The argument was that the law had been broken because YCA had a road permit from UK to Italy via France but had sailed the boats from the UK. Eric pointed out that there was no road across the Channel – he maintains that in the heat of translation he managed not to call it the English Channel. The retort was that the boats should have been transported on wheels on a ferry boat.

Every man's hand seemed to be against them now. Not only had they broken the strike, but they were also clearly avoiding giving business to the ferry operations. They were told that they could either pay £300 now and the boats would be free to move, or go to court in Dieppe in a few weeks' time and meanwhile the boats would be 'looked after'. Eric produced cash. He was told that his drivers could take the boats when they arrived the next day. He said he wanted to take the boats now. They asked why. He said he was worried that maybe the price would be higher tomorrow. They were insulted and turned away with Gallic shrugs.

Finally, a friendly gendarme was introduced, who took them to the lorry and boats and said they

could follow him in his 2CV to a large lorry park. With as much outward confidence as he could muster, Eric climbed into the cab of the enormous truck accompanied by a now sulky Chantal. The engine roared into life while he desperately tried to recall how he drove a 7-ton Army truck in his late teens. The first task was to back it out complete with trailer. Somehow he managed it and was led along the narrow back streets of Calais by the little 2CV to the lorry-and-trailer park of the town. Once parked he could not find out how to turn the engine off. (Nowadays diesel vehicles switch off with the key, but until quite recently there was an engine cut-off lever … like on a boat.) He had to resort to putting the truck in high gear and stalling it with the clutch and brakes. The gendarme was a little surprised but perhaps assumed that was what English drivers did. Chantal did not speak all the way home.

Delivery trips from Brindisi had became no simpler either. During this period a delivery fleet was split due to bad weather and two of them were 'uncertain of their position'. They had no radios and only basic navigation equipment, so decided to follow aircraft condensation trails because they thought they would lead them to Corfu. Then they saw high mountains and headed for the shore straight through an Albanian minefield. They were intercepted at gunpoint by an Albanian naval boat and arrested. The crews were separated and questioned and the boats searched. The Albanians found the YCA sailing instructions and accepted that a mistake had been made. The delivery crew were given some food and a course for Corfu, escorted back through the minefield and waved on their way back to the capitalist neighbour country.

# 1979

This was a year of considerable growth, with new fleets for the existing flotilla companies and the arrival of more new companies; there were fleets all over Greece and flotillas were moving into new Mediterranean countries.

YCA added a Dodecanese route, which flew clients to Rhodes airport while most of their sailing was on the Lycean coast ... of Turkey. Conventional tourism was in its infancy in Turkey and sailing tourism almost unknown, but despite these problems YCA and other companies always enjoyed a friendly welcome in Turkey.

The brochure carried a passing reference to potential political difficulties between the countries, and during the four years that YCA had no competition in Turkey there were rumblings of problems about the route; the Greek authorities at one stage threatened not to allow sailors to board homebound flights if they had a Turkish stamp in their passport. The opening of Dalaman airport in 1982 signalled YCA's move out of Rhodes.

Also in this year the Julian Everitt-designed YCA 29 was available on the Dodecanese route and as part of other flotillas in the Ionian and Sporades.

The company's other yachts were new badged as the YCA 25, 26 and 28. The YCA 29s were specifically designed for flotilla use with (on deck) mainsheets managed on the coachroof to keep the cockpit clear and (below) holding tanks so the heads could be used in harbour.

Together with the 29s in the Dodecanese YCA had a fleet of Snapdragons in the Ionian, and another in the Saronic Gulf. There was a fleet of Mirage 26s in the Saronic and a total of three fleets of Mirage 28s, one in the Ionian and two in the Sporades.

FSC had fleets throughout the Ionian, and this was the year that a Kiwi engineer called Barrie Neilson joined the company – he was eventually to become its owner, as Sailing Holidays. He arrived in the autumn as part of a delivery crew and found 'sixty-five boats lined up in the Old Port in Corfu, pretty neglected. So we started work – what can you do?' The existing team was still affected by Thomas's death and found it hard to accept the new crews. There was an additional problem for the winter refit in that local engineers had shaved the engine cylinder heads of the Petter engines on the Westerlies to 'cure' oil leaks, so that the pistons wouldn't turn over, and the engines had to be shimmed.

*Left* Departure preparations at Rhodes. *M. Storey*

*Right* The YCA 29: the first yacht to be specifically designed for flotilla use. *YCA*

# The new YCA 29

For the past **five years** we have been searching for the ideal **Mediterranean 'Holiday Yacht'**. During the autumn of 1976 we came to the conclusion that there was no boat available that completely met our requirements. There were boats being produced that would make good Mediterranean cruising yachts provided we incorporated **various modifications**. We were loathe to adopt this policy of compromise for our long term planning. A decision was therefore made to commission a **specialist design team** to develop a yacht **custom designed and built for YCA Mediterranean cruising**.

The result of two years hard thinking and work is the **Julian Everitt** design team's **YCA 29 'Holiday Yacht'**. The brief given to Julian was long and detailed. We wanted a boat with attractive, modern lines that would be forgiving in inexperienced hands but, when handled well, would have a performance to match her good looks. She must be easy to live aboard in sunny climes. Good ventilation and plenty of space in the saloon. Decks that are uncluttered with ample room for sunbathing and a cockpit that's as good for relaxing in as it is for sailing.

Two prototypes of **YCA 29** went down to the 'Med' as Pilot Yachts earlier this year and have been on test with our most senior sailing staff living aboard them for the **whole of the summer**.

Some idea of the attention we have paid to the details of this project can be judged when we list over 114 minor modifications incorporated into *Merlin VII*, the **YCA 29** that made her first public appearance at the **1978 Southampton Boat Show**.

Special features of this boat include a main sheeting system on the coach roof which eliminates the slide and sheets cluttering the cockpit. The mounting of her foresail winches leaves the cockpit side-decks completely clear for sitting out in the sun. This has a dual advantage below in the saloon giving excellent access to the quarter berth on the starboard side and **providing large working surfaces in the galley** to port.

A special pulpit designed for easy boarding when the yacht is moored Mediterranean style, bows to the quay. Also a **separate kedge anchor locker and warp roller** over the stern quarter to assist when mooring in this way.

The divided pushpit at the stern gives access to the **dinghy boarding ladder**. This can also be lowered below the water line for easy boarding after swimming.

Her saloon table allows seven, yes seven people, to dine in comfort but is stowed away completely out of sight when not in use. No flaps, clips, springs or sky hooks to drive you frantic and you can still serve from the galley with the table in situ.

There are two singles or a double, if you use the infill, in the fore peak. A very large quarter berth that could even be used as a double for two children. Also in the saloon there is a quickly assembled double berth to starboard and a 6' 6" single to port.

The main anchor well is designed for efficiently stowing a Bruce anchor and the fifty gallon capacity fresh water and large capacity fuel tanks are fitted with sight glasses to avoid the inconvenience of dipping. YCA 29 also has a **sewerage holding tank** so that the heads can be used in harbour. We are not going to tell you very much about our new 29's performance for two reasons. Firstly, we want you to be the judge with no preconceived ideas. Secondly, we don't want to embarrass our many friends in the boat building industry who supplied us with our existing fleets that YCA 29 will ultimately replace. We will however, guarantee you a hoilday yacht that is very well balanced and responsive, light on the helm and as much fun to sail as she is to lie on in the sun.

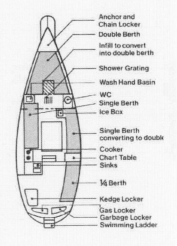

Anchor and Chain Locker
Double Berth
Infill to convert into double berth
Shower Grating
Wash Hand Basin
WC
Single Berth
Ice Box
Single Berth converting to double
Cooker
Chart Table
Sinks
¼ Berth
Kedge Locker
Gas Locker
Garbage Locker
Swimming Ladder

| Specification | |
|---|---|
| Length Overall | 29' |
| Beam | 9' 10" |
| Draft | 5' |
| Ballast | 2,750 lb |
| Displacement | 6,600 lb |
| Headroom—Saloon | 6' 1" |
| Mainsail | 144 sq ft |
| Working Jib | 152 sq ft |
| Genoa | 256 sq ft |
| Engine | Yanmar Diesel |
| Berths | 6 Full Length |

29

*Left* YCA 29s being built at
Eastbourne. *YCA*

*Middle* A YCA 29 near Marmaris
in 1980. *YCA*

*Bottom* Sunset at Epidavros in
April 1978. *YCA*

### New companies and other growth in 1979

- Tim Stevens from FSC launched his own programme, **Seven Seas Sailing**, in Yugoslavia.
- **CPT** moved ten boats (half its fleet) to Levkas.
- **Mirage Holidays** had several fleets in the Saronic.
- **Seascape** had taken the next step towards bigger boats by introducing fleets of Sadler 32s with Moody 40s as lead-boats in the Ionian.
- Tony Nielsen of **MCS** had resurfaced with a fleet of Maxi 95s and other bigger boats in Turkey.
- The first steps towards what became called 'villa flotilla' were pioneered by **Dinghy Sailing in Greece**, which offered one week in dinghies and one week on a flotilla.

# 8
# Early 1980s:
# some sailors' tales

## 1980

YCA extended the Dodecanese route with two fleets of 29s, but warned in the brochure that the sailing was more vigorous there.

'You should not cruise this area if your sailing experience is very limited. As a guide if you have cruised our Ionian or Sporadic areas and graduated to the Sporades you should be ready to enjoy sailing in the Dodecanese.'

By the early 1980s there were 400 flotilla yachts in operation, including the first French-built boats, though YCA bought two fleets of Sigma 33s. Reefing headsails and holding tanks on the boats were the latest luxuries.

---

*B*ill and Ann Melville came from New Zealand to a holiday with the Flotilla Sailing Club during September and October 1980. Their account of their time in Greece includes visits to many of the places that are the core of flotilla routes to this day. But notice the changes: they were the only boat in Vasiliki, and one of only two boats in Kioni. Moreover, in 1980 music and dancing in the villages still meant traditional music and local dancing rather than the sounds from the telly in the corner.

'To get to the flotilla base in Corfu from NZ in time was, to say the least, quite an exercise in logistics, made all the more difficult by sundry aircraft delays. We travelled from Auckland to Melbourne to Singapore to Bahrain to Damascus to Frankfurt to Athens to Corfu, arriving just in time to catch the flotilla group to ferry us to Igoumenitsa and then be bussed down the coast to the base at Levkas where our Jaguar 27 *Leros* awaited us. Crazy!! Yes, but what the hell, we were young!!

The passage plan for the fourteen days, which included about five days free sailing, was Levkas-Nidri-Sivota (on Levkas)-Fiscardo-Kioni-Vasiliki-Spiglia-Gaios-Mongonissi-Lakka-Sivota (on mainland Greece)-Petreti-Gouvia Marina, Corfu. I think the costs were about £250 per person.

The rest of the flotilla crews arrived from Gatwick and seemed rather bemused as to why on earth we would travel half way round the world when sailing in our own backyard seemed to them so much better. For us to sail in an area so steeped in history and experience the culture, friendliness, music and dancing in an area so divorced from the so-called sophistication of our day-to-day existence was a memorable time still remembered with fondness. Also the sailing was relaxing apart from one rather fresh day – the sun shone – the sea was warm – the Domestica was cheap and the food was great. What more can one wish for?

Many of the crews of the other thirteen boats in the flotilla seemed intent on getting to the next port as soon as possible in order to get a good spot close to the

*Left* Petriti, Corfu, in October 1980. *Bill Melville*

*Left* Jaguars at Sivota Mourtos back anchorage in 1980. *Sailing Holidays*

*Below* The Jaguar flotilla – including the Melvilles' boat – at Fiscardo. *Bill Melville*

Vasiliki in 1980. *Both Bill Melville*

taverna, with the danger of running out of fuel before the next place where it was available. We sailed on, stopping for lunch and a swim and arriving last at the next port so many times we were presented with The Wooden Spoon at the farewell dinner at Gouvia. (We still use the spoon on our own boat.)

We experienced the ire of the Port Captain at Vasiliki for not flying the Greek flag. Being the only boat in the port I suspect the old gentleman sitting with his worry beads outside the taverna, who insisted on taking our bow lines as we approached the harbour wall, apprised the authorities of this fact when I neglected to buy him an ouzo. Later I felt quite mean for not having done so. The Port Captain, whose command of

English was on a par with my Greek, demanded to know from whence we came and whither we goeth, and if we ever returned not flying the Greek flag woe betide us – he then gave a dramatic thumbs down gesture. In spite of this rather shaky start we found Vasiliki to be delightfully unspoiled – just as we imagined a small Greek fishing village to be – fishermen mending their nets – pressing grapes – buying fresh bread from a blackened oven used for generations.

Further memories:
- Sivota (Levkas): A rather basic taverna on the harbour edge with a rather large crab in the water tied by the claw to its cage awaiting the whim of a passing diner.

- Kioni (Ithica): Just us and a Fisher 31 in the bay – walking up the hill behind the port past a small school in class with the windows open and calling 'Kalimera' and the school teacher replying 'Good morning'.
- Spiglia (Meganisi): Climbing the steep road to a taverna in the village above and looking back down at the moored flotilla.
- Gaios (Paxos): A busy port – a bit touristy with evidence of previous conflict from the bullet holes in some of the walls.
- Anti-Paxos: A beautiful bay on the NE corner – crystal clear warm water – a small building on the foreshore and only one other boat in the bay – heavenly.
- Petriti (Corfu): A small rather shallow port (as some found out) with few facilities and a taverna filled with several drunken fishermen who insisted on dancing with yours truly!!! And the look of disapproval from the kitchen staff at the spectacle of a female crew member from the flotilla joining in the line of men dancing.

Altogether a wonderful sailing, cultural experience – I wonder if we would be disappointed if we returned after twenty-seven years... We still receive Sailing Holidays brochures to whet the appetite.'

*Above* Gaios (Paxos): the town quay in 1980. *Sailing Holidays*

*Below* Bill Melville relaxing. *Bill Melville*

## 1981

This year there were a number of new offerings from YCA: a Cyclades cruise (limited to early and late season because of the strong winds in July and August), charters of a 37-foot yacht in the Grenadine Islands through a partnership with Caribbean Sailing Yachts, and 'Clubhouse' dinghy sailing at Nidri.

The latter was based on a beach hotel looking towards Meganisi and Scorpios, where up to forty people could be accommodated. Wanderer and Laser dinghies were available in the first year, with Hobie cats arriving subsequently.

*Right* A detailed chart showing beaches and other possible landing places from Nidri to the north of Meganisi, prepared for the 'Clubhouse' sailors using Wanderer dinghies. *YCA*

*Right* The beach at Nidri and the YCA Clubhouse. *K. Thompson*

*I*n 1982 **Joan Gould** published in the *New York Times* an account of her time in a YCA Snapdragon, which she titled 'Sailing the Wine-Dark Seas'. She had joined YCA flotillas in the Saronic Gulf in two previous years.

She refers to herself as 'a day sailor and racer (and, let's be frank … a middle-aged suburban woman)'. Her written style and the delight she takes in her Greek experience (including the privations of sharing with two other adults a 25-foot sloop with no holding tank) and the passing remark that 'I've skippered my own racing boat for more than twenty years on Long Island Sound, and know a fair amount about jibing spinnakers' show her to be a more impressive person than she pretends.

She calls the Snapdragon 'a stocky little vessel, sturdy as a jeep and just about as luxurious.' She reminds us that 'when we wash ourselves, our dishes, occasionally even our clothes, we do so thriftily, since every ounce of fresh water has to be lugged aboard in plastic jugs.' The food is new to her, including 'the raw cucumber sprinkled with pepper that we take with our ouzo, another proof that we're not where – or even what – we were a few weeks ago,' though the cost of the meal including wine 'almost never comes to more than $6 a person, including tip.'

I should have liked to include a large excerpt from Joan's writing, but have been unable to find anyone to give me permission. Joan has a website, which includes a charming photo of a woman in her seventies who looks thoroughly capable of sailing her own yacht. Mails and faxes to the agents listed have only referred me to other agents who don't reply at all. A company that handles reprints from the *New York Times* seemed quite unable to discover whether they owned the copyright to the item, but could tell me the minimum fee just in case they did. So here is the link to type into your browser if you'd like to see the whole article: http://query.nytimes.com/gst/fullpage.html?sec=travel&res=9C0CE4DB1138F934A25752C0A9 64948260. Alternatively Google 'sailing the wine dark seas flotilla'.

Here is a sample of Joan's writing about flotilla sailing:

'The concept, when I first heard it several years ago, struck me with the brilliance of Aegean light refracted from a whitewashed wall: I could go sailing in those "wine-dark seas" where barren rocks stand forth as clear and compelling as the columns of the Parthenon – but I could also go sightseeing, to places like the beehive tomb of Agamemnon, where an insect buzzing in that pinnacle of darkness would sound in my ears like the hum of death itself.

I could skipper a small boat, not so different from my own day racer, in the Mediterranean, but I could rely on a sailing master to see to it that I didn't get stuck forever in some uninhabited cove because I didn't know how to get my anchor line out from under a rock. Saying no to such a proposition would be like locking myself in the boat's cabin while a summer southerly is blowing, with full sails set.'

'A stocky little vessel, sturdy as a jeep and just about as luxurious.' *YCA*

*I*an Meikle, his wife Hazel, his seven-year-old son and his friend Geoff sailed in the Ionian with YCA in late May 1983, and their account describes some things that were very similar to the Melvilles' experience three years earlier, and some that had changed. This was the second year that it was possible to fly into Preveza. The account of windsurfing at Fiscardo is perhaps the most startling to those who have been there from the 1990s onwards, though the notion that there were just three mooring spots at Sivota is eye-catching too. Ian refers to Zaverda as the port where they left the boats; this is the village now known as Paleros. YCA changeovers were still on Wednesdays.

'We flew from Gatwick to Preveza. There was a small civil terminal building mainly used for arrivals. Departures were from a garden area just outside the terminal building. We boarded a bus and travelled north to Parga. On the way the coach had to reverse onto the ferry to cross Preveza harbour, and the coast road was very narrow with mountains on one side and steep drops to the sea on the other. It was quite late before we made another ferry crossing to Gayos on Paxos where we were shown to our YCA 29, *Diadem*.

The next morning after the briefing we went shopping and had lunch in the cockpit. We were delayed by harbour controls, but at 2.30, although it was blowing force 5-6, we set out for Lakka in the north of the island. The weather proved too much for some boat crews so we turned tail and ran before the wind down to Mongonissi Bay at the foot of Paxos, arriving at 6.00. We ate that evening at the only taverna on a beautiful enclosed bay. The following morning we sailed to Anti-Paxos and anchored for lunch and a swim at a beach then sailed back to Mongonissi for another evening at the taverna there, where we dined on lobster.

On Saturday we sailed for Parga. Winds were light so we motorsailed part of the way, mooring on the quay just inside the sea

The quay at Mongonissi. *Ian Meikle*

Parga from the Venetian Castle.
*YCA*

The YCA flotilla that Ian joined,
at Parga. *Ian Meikle*

wall. The water in the bay was brown due to olive pressing in the hills above the bay. In the evening we took a small local boat into Parga where we dined, before catching the 10.30pm boat back to our berth. Sunday was a day of rest, and the water in the bay had cleared. Geoff and I went paragliding around the bay from a lovely sandy beach. Snorkelling and swimming off the rocks on the opposite side of the jetty was a must.

Next day we sailed for the Lefkas Canal, stopping for a swim on the way. The weather was calm and the whole flotilla stopped and drifted for a while. At 4.00 we entered the canal and motored through, arriving at Nidri after 6.00. We anchored in the bay off the point where the YCA had a

base, and dinghied ashore to have showers at the YCA club and change travellers' cheques. We ate at Nick the Greek's restaurant. The following morning my wife found a taverna with a washing machine and managed to get our washing done.

The following day we sailed for Meganisi Island and Port Spiglia, a lovely spot with no tavernas. We had to walk up the winding road to the village of Spartahori where there was a view site looking over the bay. We four dined and drank all evening for £10, at Billy the Chicken's Bar.

Next day we visited Port Vathy en route to comb the shore for driftwood for the barbecue to be held when we anchored in Abeliki Bay. There we had a feast prepared

Ian Meikle and the YCA 29 *Diadem* in the Meganisi Channel in 1983. *Ian Meikle*

for us by our lead-boat's crew, and built a big fire to cook our food on in the sand, paddling back to our boats in the darkness at 1.30am.

On Thursday we rounded Meganisi, stopping for lunch at the island of Atoko, and on to Vathi on Ithaka where we anchored in a bay near to Gregory's Taverna. We had dinner ashore, then walked into the town for coffee, taking a taxi back and turning in at midnight. The wind was rising and at 2.30am we kept anchor watch. Anchors on the other boats were dragging during the night and the lead-boat crew had to man their dinghy and rescue several boats that were drifting away. Our anchor held but the lead-boat with only the hostess on board drifted down on to us and we had to reset her anchor after catching her as she drifted into our port side.

In the morning we went alongside the quay and took on fresh water from a tanker truck that was passing. The Port Authorities advised us not to sail, though they wanted us to move away from the main town quay, so we returned to the anchorage and ate at Gregory's where he roasted a lamb over a spit. On Saturday the wind was still high so we walked into Vathi and did some shopping. By the evening the sea was calmer and the wind had decreased.

On Sunday we set out for Cephalonia in calm seas with little wind to Fiscardo Bay. This was a very pleasant spot with a single row of tavernas and all thirteen boats moored outside the Captain's Cabin, where we had lunch. We spent the afternoon swimming and windsurfing and I managed to get out into the bay, only to have to be towed back by a fishing-boat. The water was very clean. In the village we bought fresh bread from the baker and really enjoyed the peace of the place. That

Vathi on Meganisi in 1983. Janet Welch, who sent me this picture and a good many others that I've used, has been visiting the Ionian for twenty-five years. When this picture was taken she remembers seeing a little old lady throwing her cooking pots into the harbour: Janet assumes it was a domestic tiff.

Of the Ionian in general she says, 'I'm afraid the stately pace of life has gone, although fortunately not all the charm. The Greeks are as lovely as ever!' She wonders why harbours have been developed by infilling rather than dredging, and finds it 'tiresome to have to make sure we tie up by early afternoon in some ports in order to make sure we can get in. Even in late May Kioni was "full" on several nights, ditto Vathy on Meganissi.' Nevertheless she continues to come. *Gordon Sharp*

evening we dined at George Theorem's Taverna and staggered in at 12.30am.

Sailing back northwards we called in at Sivota. There was just room for three boats on the quay and everyone else rafted off. We had the final dinner before sailing to Zaverda, our final port. From off Nidri we were supposed to race without the use of the engine, but using any other means of propulsion. At first we were in the lead but the wind died away and we tried swimming ahead with a rope pulling the boat, and towing it with the dinghy. Others made oars and some put the engine out of gear and turned the prop on the crank. The race ended with everyone motoring around throwing buckets of water at each other.

On arrival at Zaverda we had to clean the boats and have an inspection. We dined at a taverna by the beach under a vine-covered pergola, then back to the boat to pack our belongings.

At 6.30 the following morning we were bussed back to the airport at Preveza, on the way stopping for breakfast at Vonitsa, then checked in at the airport where we waited in the departure lounge, the garden outside, for our charter flight home to Gatwick.'

# Operations Manager

During the 1970s the lead-crews were often recruited because they were on the spot and competent, and those who were part of the flotillas then remember the experience with great warmth as well as wonder that everything actually went on working. By the end of the '80s everything was on a more professional basis, although a main criterion for the crews on the spot continued to be reliability and enthusiasm.

This description of the job of the Operations Manager is taken from a YCA newsletter in 1983:

'The year really starts in the autumn when he organises the winter lay-up for our fleets and decides about the refurbishing work that will have to be done before the next season and also what we will need to purchase. Laying up the boats has its amusing moments, as in Marmaris last year when our Turkish friends enthusiastically encouraged us to bring all thirty-six boats ashore at their new "boat yard"! We did not realise at the time that their facilities were limited to the one primitive fisherman's sledge, worked by winch hawser and muscle-power. What the locals lacked in technology they soon made up for in old-fashioned skills and an ability for hard work.

During the winter he usually has some special projects to accomplish. Last winter it was decided that YCA policy was to have holding tanks fitted to all boats. It was his responsibility to organise the purchasing of this equipment, supervising the production of prototype tanks and finally dispatching the staff teams to do the job. Because it is virtually impossible to purchase yacht equipment to the correct standard in our

Winter lay-up. *YCA*

Over-winter damage like this lightning-strike at Levkas was thankfully rare. *Both YCA*

cruising areas, the most simple tasks must be planned to literally the last nut and bolt, not forgetting the extras for those that get dropped down the bilges.

Once we decide, in the late summer, where each of our eleven fleets will operate the following year and what boats are to be replaced, he plans the best method of positioning them to their summer cruising grounds. He also organises our road transport to deliver new yachts from the UK to Brindisi, our base in Italy.

He decides what delivery cruises are to be revenue-earning and sold as Spring Cruises, but at the same time ensuring that we have enough early season sailing to give to our volunteer refit teams as a "thank you" for their hard work.

Once he has planned the start of the new season's operations, he prepares a written

diary that explains to every YCA staff member, our agents and all other interested parties precisely who is doing what on each day for this critical period from early March through to mid-May.

He is in charge of YCA sailing staff and is the key member of our selection team. We currently have thirty-seven sailing staff plus our own UK-based instructors. He gives detailed briefings to each flotilla team before they depart from the UK and then, at an early stage in the build-up to the season, travels out to the operating areas to make sure all is going to plan. If there are any hitches, he is on the spot to solve the problems as they arrive. Mid-season sees him returning once again to the fleets. It is at this time that he may diplomatically enquire which *Merlin* crews are considering signing on again for the following season.'

It became common practice to offer clients out-of-season delivery cruises: the clients gained the experience of a more extensive voyage at a limited cost, and the company gained competent crews to move boats from one area to another. Those keen enough paid their way by joining in with the pre-season work on the boats, which was not always as glamorous at it might have seemed.

# Lead-crews and restaurants

The taverna owners who worked with the flotillas in the 1970s and '80s are perfectly clear that the work was a partnership with the lead-crews. There were few places for the crew to take their group of hungry and thirsty sailors, and the facilities of the kitchens could easily be stretched too far by the arrival of a big group. The flotilla barbecue evening was originally invented to deal with this shortage of places to eat.

To see a modern lead-crew helping the staff of a restaurant to keep track of orders by boat names, or explaining what the dishes consist of to uncertain teenage vegetarians, is all the evidence needed that the partnership is still alive. In just the same way there are plenty of taverna owners who join in the responsibility for mooring boats.

If the lead-crew are part of the team it is reasonable that they help themselves to bottles of beer, that they eat as part of the family rather than as customers and that they wear the insignia of their friends' restaurants on tee-shirts or boat flags. Inside many of the tavernas are photos, signed flags or other mementos from lead-crews, thanking the Greek families for their help during an early season.

However, the conversations that were recorded for this book included some uncomfortable suggestions. They were suggestions, and some of what was said was contradictory. It would be good to think the negative suggestions were inaccurate.

A thoughtful and successful young man put it this way:

'It's not everywhere, and the managers are not aware, I believe, but some skippers take advantage. They ask for "back money" – commission for bringing customers to your place. It's not all companies, but they might say, "I bring thirty people, I need 2 euros or 3 or 5 per head." It's not fair on the local people, as that's a part of their profit, so when this happens the quality is very low. If I know we have agreed you will bring me fifty people per week, and the clients don't like the food, it will not be the same clients next time so it doesn't matter.

Hostess Jane Hannah in Turkey, 1980 – the lead-crew as part of the local family! *YCA*

*Above* Mooring a flotilla at Hydra in 1982. *A. Danielsson*

*Below* Arriving at Poros town in 1982. *H. French*

Also some tavernas are not used. [One company] spread themselves around, but some have only used one place, not bothered to try the others. I think it is not so much ignorance as laziness. Sometimes a flotilla will moor by one taverna, and the clients are sent to another place. The clients know no better. People do what the leaders say – they assume they know what is best.'

I asked other people in other ports about paying commission for bringing customers. Some told me in no uncertain terms what they would say to anyone who suggested it. One said that, far from asking for commission, she knew of lead-crews who were embarrassed by always being offered payment in a particular village.

Nevertheless I was told elsewhere that most lead-crews ask for money, like most coach drivers or most tripper-boat captains; it could be argued that this was a bitter response from someone whose business was not as successful as some others.

There's no doubt at all, though, that whether through friendship or laziness, or for some financial reason, the patronage of the flotillas in a port where there is a range of restaurants can make the difference between a successful business and a failure. One of the jobs of the hostess is to suggest good places to eat; one of the duties of the crew as a whole is continue the tradition of fairness established when the very first flotillas arrived.

## The secret of a being a good flotilla skipper

The two people quoted below were both involved in creating the role of flotilla leader in the 1970s, then went on to management roles in flotilla companies. Each of them has extensive experience and was involved in pioneering the systems we now take for granted. They spent a good many years criss-crossing each other's paths in the Mediterranean, but they never met. It is striking,

Port Symi in the Dodecanese. *YCA*

though, that in conversation about their experience of the early days they both spoke so similarly about what goes to make a good experience on a flotilla.

**Mike Cox:** 'A good skipper is someone who doesn't panic, doesn't shout. All these people arrive, and get on twelve different boats, and they're all very different people. Perhaps they've got high-powered or stressful jobs and they've had a long flight, probably been up since four in the morning, maybe had a blazing row with the family. They don't want to be told what to do and they're uptight, and they've got to sail a boat that they've gone and booked and they're not even sure they can drive it.

People will react in very different ways and they can be very rude to the staff. They'll say, "Oh, this doesn't work, that doesn't work." It does work, they just haven't done it properly, so you have to bite your tongue until they say, "Well, actually I couldn't get this to work – can you show me how to do it?"

The idea was that first of all you calmed them down, then you showed them they could sail the boat. After four or five days they'd all be chilled out. We'd watch them change. Then when they got off the boat at the end of the holiday they were all exactly the same. They were brown and relaxed and confident, and they'd had a great time.'

**Barrie Neilson:** 'The greatest reward for me and for all our flotilla crews is watching people coming off the coach quite tentatively, quite nervously, and at the end of the holiday bounding off the boat, all brown – you'd think they'd been on boats all their lives. When they talk about it they're almost gushing, absolutely full of energy; the transformation in one fortnight is almost unbelievable – confident, happy, met a whole lot of new people … you can't buy that in a can.'

Sivota in 1978.

# 9
# 1982: two new airports

This year saw two airports become available that would each have an important effect.

On 13 May 1982 an Air Europe 737 carrying 130 YCA sailors approached Dalaman Airport in Turkey. The airport was brand new and this was the very first flight. All the important local people and Turkish media were awaiting the arrival. The pilot made his approach but flew 30 feet above the runway, then climbed away again. He then made another approach and landed.

Every visitor on the first tourist flight into Dalaman airport received presents: a rose, a jar of local honey and one of these banners. *Author*

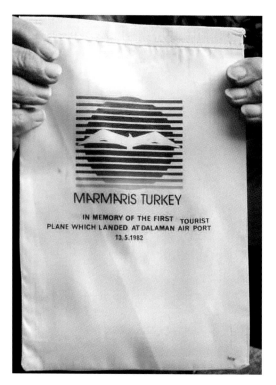

MARMARIS TURKEY

IN MEMORY OF THE FIRST TOURIST
PLANE WHICH LANDED AT DALAMAN AIR PORT
13.5.1982

Later he explained that he felt it prudent to just check that there were no dumper trucks or bags of concrete still lying about.

Customs was abandoned that day and the sailors were astonished to be greeted by thirty children in Turkish national dress. An hour later the flotilla crews climbed aboard their coaches following TV interviews for the aircraft captain, bouquets for the stewardesses and a 'crocodile' dance with musicians, the children and the airport staff. Each visitor was welcomed with a rose, a jar of local honey and a banner. This was the beginning of mass tourism in Turkey, and enabled YCA to discontinue the Rhodes connection to their Lycean coast route.

Less dramatic but an important factor in the growth of Ionian tourism generally had been the availability of Actio Airport at Prevesa. Preveza was (and still is) a military airport, and it was some years before a complete terminal building appeared. Not until the new century was there a substantial modern building with air- conditioning. The arrangements for the first years can be imagined from the title given to the airport by the transfer staff: Olive Tree Airport. The YCA brochure says 'it's definitely much more fun than Gatwick', though Gatwick in those days was definitely much less fun even than nowadays.

The important change though was that it became possible for flotillas to be based south of the Levkas Canal: in the heart of the area that the early surveys identified as most suitable. Some of the flotilla operators regard this as the turning-point for flotillas in the Ionian, and the saving of the area as a major flotilla area: 'If someone had a bad transfer and lost a day in a hotel they probably wouldn't be

*Above* Port Atheni, Meganisi, in 1978. *Sailing Holidays*

*Below* Waterfront reflections at Marmaris in 1980. *T. Simpson*

put off sailing or flotillas but they'd very likely go to a different area next time.'

YCA used Levkas Town for some changeovers in 1982 and moved to Vasiliki in 1983. Companies like FSC, which had established bases on Corfu, retained them, but as time went on they increasingly offered cruises alternating between Corfu to Levkas and Levkas to Corfu. Levkas Island in general became accessible for land-based tourism, and the infrastructure that this brought to Levkas Town, Nidri, Sivota and Vasiliki enabled a second wave of changes. The flotillas from 1976 to 1982 had introduced the villages and the tavernas to the possibility of tourist business, but the big changes on land happened over the next ten years. In 1982 Sivota was described as 'almost untouched by progress' and Nidri was said to have 'some good beach-side tavernas'. By 1992 Sivota had its present concrete quay and many of the present restaurants, and at Nidri the row of bars and coffee shops between the ferry berth and the beach was in place much as today.

As a result of its more southern base, YCA describes a flotilla route including Ay Eufemia and Porus on Cephalonia, and also Zante. The latter turned out not to be popular: it was a long journey to Zante Town, which was not a particularly attractive destination anyway. This journey was a rare occasion when the yachts might be set off their course (westward) by a current.

Extended use of Cephalonian ports remained on the itineraries though, and Fiscardo began to move from the periphery; in 1982 it was still 'a sleepy haven with just two tavernas'. Its own growth really took off as Argostoli airport was developed.

Sigma 33s (YCA 33) were available on the Lycean Coast Flotillas.

The year 1982 saw Sail America, a company set up by Des Pollard, who built the Jaguars, offering flotillas in the Florida Keys. Barrie Neilson was the skipper. He had been a skipper for FCS since the middle of the 1980 season, and he wrote a guide to the new area and ran the boats. Des's mistake was not to market the flotillas to the Americans; the transatlantic trade suffered during this year when the first batch of cheap flights offered by the likes of Freddie Laker and Air Florida ran into trouble. One of the Jaguars was afloat in Florida very recently – a bilge-keel boat (built for Southend!) called *Fay*.

*Left* Barrie Neilson running a briefing in Florida – some clients are more absorbed than others.
*Sailing Holidays*

# 10
# The mid-1980s and onwards

Flotilla sailing had grown from a precarious idea operated by a tiny team of amateurs on the periphery of the travel industry to an established part of both the leisure and the yachting worlds. Just ten years after the first flotilla boats were denied space at Earls Court, the 1983 Boat Show seemed to have as many stands selling holidays as boats. In the late 1980s *Yachting World* began a special supplement called 'Charter World'. (Note the smarter concept 'charter', although much of the content was about flotillas, or boats and facilities available from flotilla companies.)

The YCA stand at Earls Court in 1981. In that year a major boat-building company had gone into receivership and the flotilla company took over the large stand at short notice. What a contrast with the 1974 show, when the best that could be managed for this unregarded fledgling concept was to hand out leaflets in the street outside. *YCA*

## 1983–84

- **Yugoslavia** was now established as a destination and YCA had flotillas of Sigma 33s there. They had fitted roller-reefing genoas to all their boats, and holding tanks in all except the Snapdragons. The reunions that had seemed so appropriate in 1974 when there were very small numbers of clients were still going strong, and the company was now offering a 'rail deal' with prices inclusive of rail travel to and from Gatwick.
- **Greeksail** and **Mediterranean Charter Services** were bought by Guinness.

- **Dinghy Sailing in Greece** joined with the large Falcon Leisure Services group and became **Falcon Sailing Holidays**.
- **Mirage Holidays** and **Yachtours** ceased trading.
- YCA acquired **Seascape**'s yachts.
- Guinness later sold off its sailing holiday business, which became **Island Sailing** who in turn bought **Seven Seas Sailing Holidays**.

This left three big groupings: YCA, Island Sailing and Falcon Sailing. **Flotilla Sailing Club** remained independent and continued to focus on the Ionian area.

## Mergers and name changes

The diagram below is intended to show how some of the early flotilla companies changed their names or merged. It is not intended to show business development; some of the new groupings were the result of formal takeovers or amalgamations, but some followed bankruptcy and others resulted from quite informal changes of name. Nor is it possible to show every company, even those that traded before 1980, or to be precise about whether boats sold by a closing business meant that the old company had been taken over or just some of its assets. Finally, the diagram by no means attempts to trace the backgrounds of the huge multinational travel businesses whose umbrellas now shelter most of the offspring of those original tiny companies.

| | | | | |
|---|---|---|---|---|
| 1974 | YCA | | | |
| 1975 | | | | |
| 1976 | | MCS | | |
| 1977 | | | | |
| 1978 | | | Greeksail | |
| 1979 | | in Turkey | | Seven Sea |
| 1980 | Bought by Guinness | | | |
| Mid 1980s | Sold: becomes Island Sailing | | | Bought by Isl |
| 1987 | YCA sold; later bought by Island Group becomes Sunsail | | | |
| 1990 | | | | |
| Post-1990 | | | | |

*Above* Anchoring. *C. Richards*

*Below* A Moody 34 (centre-cockpit) under cruising chute. *YCA*

*Above* YCA's Eric Richardson at the Boat Show with the Turkish Ambassador. *YCA*

| GIYH | | | | |
|------|------|------|------|------|
| FSC | | | | |
| | CPT | | | |
| | | Dinghy Sailing in Greece | Mirage | Seascape |
| | | | | |
| | Joins with Falcon Group | | Closes | Closes (boats to YCA) |
| | | | | |
| ing Holidays | | | | |
| | Sovereign/Sun World/Neilson | | | |

The general recession in business brought about takeovers, mergers and some weeding out of companies, but the overall expansion of the market in these holidays continued.

By the end of the decade these bigger groupings were beginning to influence the yacht-building industry. In the early days the first companies had to search for builders with the imagination and capacity to accept an order for a dozen boats at a time and look for second-hand yachts to make up their numbers. By contrast, at the end of this decade it was possible to see the flotilla companies becoming the major customers of the boat-builders, and whole ranges of yachts being designed specifically to their requirements. A small number of yacht-designers would continue to produce high-priced and individual yachts with snug cabins from which their owners could look out at the damp weather of northern Europe.

The YCA 29 was available with flotillas in 1979; that this specially designed boat was specified, built and delivered in only the sixth flotilla season shows how quickly Eric Richardson and his team had spotted that space, ventilation, ease of maintenance and ease of handling needed to be maximised. As an engineer said, 'So long as the engine works and the heads works everyone's happy.'

In its 1987 brochure YCA spoke of a 'Buy British' policy when referring to its new Moody range, and in the same paragraph described what was already becoming standard practice,

> '…to have only one type of yacht operating in a particular flotilla. With a mixed flotilla some people, to avoid being left behind, will have to spend much of the day under power and this is not our idea of enjoyable cruising.'

By this time all new boats, whichever the company, had a three-cabin layout. FSC had Beneteau 345s in the Ionian from 1985, and Island Sailing was using Beneteaus in Turkey: 'Buy British' as a slogan became 'Buy French' as a practicality during the next decade.

Brochures from 1987 still referred to Actio airport as 'Olive Tree Airport' and said that maybe there would be a terminal next year.

## Flotilla Sailing Club to Sailing Holidays

Between the 1985 and 1990 seasons FSC went through a series of changes that could have brought it the same fate as the majority of the original companies. In 1983 Barrie Neilson had taken six boats to Yugoslavia for FSC; in 1984 there was a full flotilla of twelve boats there. The lead-crew had to consist of skipper/engineer plus hostess, since the government required there to be a 'minder' too. The bulk of the company's boats continued to be based in the Ionian.

Tom Keen had been advised to spend £2,000,000 on a batch of brand new Beneteau 345s, and an attempt was made to set up a sort of Club Med in Abelike Bay. The 345s were eventually sold in 2000, when new Beneteaus were bought. They were much loved, and a lot of work was done to improve them over the fifteen years the company ran them, including adding swimming platforms to the forward-sloping transoms. Several of them are still to be seen in the hands of private owners in Greece, but they were not ideal for flotilla use, having tillers when clients preferred wheels, and needing self-tailing winches and mainsail furling.

During the 1985 season the new boats were used on a one-way route between Zante and Corfu. Flights were complicated to arrange, but it was possible; nevertheless bookings were poor and it became clear that the investment would lose money. Staff in Greece and in London lost their jobs and Tom's health was failing.

At the end of the season Barrie Neilson formed a partnership to buy the company over a period of years. Bookings improved but the partnership was not a success and Barrie spent two years in the UK building a 41-foot yacht until in 1990 he and his wife Heidi were able to take on full responsibility for the flotillas. They had registered 'Sailing Holidays' as a company name and determined that the only way to restore Tom's standards by instituting proper maintenance and sales processes was to do it themselves: 'No bludgers'.

Although the Sailing Holidays fleet now includes about 160 boats, most of them modern, Barry is proud that the 345s, and of course the

*Above* Beneteau 345s in Mourtos Bay in 1985. This photo was taken from almost the same location as the 1979 shot on page 45 and shows Yannis's taverna. *Sailing Holidays*

*Right* Barrie Neilson and Heidi at Rovinj in Yugoslavia in 1983. They formed a partnership in 1985 to buy FSC. *Sailing Holidays*

Another view of Beneteau 345s at Mourtos. This picture was used for the cover of the FSC brochure in 1985, and shows the extended quay and road half built. It was taken on the same day as the one on the previous page, but from the hillside behind Yannis's taverna, looking back towards the town quay. *Sailing Holidays*

Jaguars originally purchased in the late 1970s, have had such a long working life. Careful servicing and maintenance over the whole period with the company has enabled a range of holiday styles to be offered. Jaguars are still with the company by public request; there is a firm market for a smaller boat, and new boats get a bit bigger every year.

## Bureaucracy or politics?

Setting up a business of this kind in Greece in the 1970s had not been simple. It happened that British financial law worked in favour of a flotilla company: 100% capital allowances, designed to help companies installing machinery in a factory, applied equally to yachts purchased as part of a business venture.

However, Greece was just emerging from a very controlling right-wing government, and local officials had relatively little experience of using their initiative. On the one hand they were fiercely proud of their country's independence, while on the other there was the tradition of hospitality to strangers. When the man on the spot was dealing with a flotilla company, should he react as if to a friendly young yachtsman, maybe from as far away as New Zealand, who was doing his best and spoke only a few comical words of Greek, or should he lay down the letter of the law to keep foreign capitalists in their place?

In addition, during the late '70s there was a campaign in parts of the Greek press to question whether tourists should be able to sail around in foreign-owned boats. The argument was they were enjoying the natural environment of Greece without contributing to the local economy though taxes. The flotilla companies suspected that this campaign was orchestrated by owners of Greek companies offering luxury crewed yachts for charter to very rich foreigners; charters of this sort were going through a bad patch because of international politics.

The opening salvo was an article in March 1978. It referred to 'a huge scandal with multinational ramifications' and said 'thousands of dollars in hire are being paid abroad so that tourists will come to Greece and appear as guests of the owners of the yachts'. Later on it said that 'Mr Henry Ford the well-know automobile king' came on such a yacht last August, that 'Edward Kennedy and Mrs Bird Johnson' were expected this year and 'the famous Mick Jagger came last year after paying US$25,000 for a 23-day cruise', but the yacht 'did not have the courage to come to Greece'.

There was of course no real overlap between the sort of people who enjoyed a holiday with two others in a 25-foot Snapdragon and the potential charterer of a 100-foot-plus yacht complete with crew, cooks and butler. Nevertheless, on one famous occasion there was a headline in the press that roughly translated as 'Richardson the Pirate! He steals our water and our sunshine!' with a photo of a Greek Navy officer with binoculars searching the horizon for that pirate.

A good deal of energy was expended in the late 1970s and early '80s attempting to make the points that the flotilla companies were bringing tourists to Greece without requiring the local economy to provide expensive infrastructure and that this was of real benefit to far-flung villages and islands.

YCA bore the brunt of the press campaign, but those running the companies twenty-five years later make the same point today about the benign effects of the flotilla industry. Barry Neilson says:

'Sailing Holidays brings 7,000 people per year to Greece. Each of them spends perhaps £30 per day on food, drinks, presents and so on – £30 times 14 days equals £420, times 7,000 equals £2.95 million brought into the local economy, besides what the companies themselves spend on fuel and any spares and equipment they buy locally. That's with a negligible carbon footprint – no big concrete buildings, hotels and swimming pools.'

In the mid-1970s a new Greek law forced all flotilla boats to sail under the Greek flag, and companies had to be Greek-owned. Photis Demas continued

Eric Richardson: not very piratical! *Eric Richardson*

to be the Greek face of YCA, 'keeping all the books in his office and wrangling with the Greek tax man.'

For whatever reason, Customs officials at local ports of entry were not expecting to deal with small yachts arriving on apparently commercial errands, and the regulations regarded them as cargo ships. Anyone who has been a flotilla client will be familiar with the notion of receiving the 'boat papers' before setting off, and know that the company chartering the boat has to complete the papers once the client is in Greece, then get the papers officially stamped. The paperwork was even more complex in the mid-'70s; Mike Cox of YCA says that he had to become an expert on Greek maritime law to manage the comings and goings at all.

Another problem, this time political with a capital P, was the Turkish connection. Greece and Turkey were at war in 1974, and the question of the

*Above* Plaka village quay. *P. Edgson Wright*

*Below* The impounded boats at Corfu, with the equipment stowed on the quay. *YCA*

sovereignty of Cyprus has persisted well into the 21st century. Some sorts of tourism can override national boundaries, however, and from 1979 until 1981 YCA was working with both countries, including running a flotilla that brought the clients to the Greek airport in Rhodes and sailing with them to the Turkish coast – good for the two local economies, good for the tourists, but not comfortable for national sensibilities on the big scale.

These issues led to confusions minor and major. Eric Richardson was twice arrested in Greece on suspicion of spying while taking photos from a dinghy to prepare a survey for the flotillas. Another time two Turkish policemen attached themselves to Eric in circumstances that he found concerning and followed him everywhere; it turned out that they had been told to give him all the help they could but weren't sure what sort of help would be appropriate.

There was a much more serious outcome in the spring of 1983 when a group of eight boats being delivered from Brindisi was impounded by the Customs at Corfu because it was carrying spares and other equipment, and the skippers spent a week in jail as smugglers. The fines and the loss of the boats and gear were a major blow for YCA. At the end of the season there were allegations that the boats at Rhodes were breaking maritime law because of the lack of safety equipment. The allegation didn't stick, partly because all the boats had very recently been thoroughly checked by the port police, and partly because they were ashore for the winter and all their safety equipment was stored in a shed.

Amongst those who were working in the flotilla companies then, the events of 1983 at Corfu between officialdom and YCA are well-known, though everyone knows a different version of just what happened and why. Was it all just a 'stuff-up' – muddles between people on the spot who didn't understand what was going on? Or was it a concerted effort to attack the leading foreign company in a new and lucrative business? Whatever the reason, the loss of the boats and equipment and the fines paid to free the crews hit YCA hard just at the point when flotilla holidays were established and beginning to move centre-stage in the holiday business and the yachting industry.

# Island Sailing and YCA to Sunsail

Greeksail was now owned by the Guinness group (one of that company's diversifications into the leisure market), and was run from Hayling Island. The Emsworth Sailing School, a few miles down the coast in Chichester Harbour, happened to use the same printers to produce its brochures. Through this introduction Chris Gordon, who ran the sailing school, was in a position to take over the flotilla operation when Guinness wanted to sell in 1982.

Chris, then aged 27, had previously set up a sailing school in Poole Harbour, which he ran with his father, but had struck out on his own when he and his wife took over the school at Emsworth. They had been involved in a flotilla cruising venture in the Bahamas, which had been too small to be viable, but the forty-eight boats from Greeksail and another fifty bought in the next two years, together with the fleet from Seven Seas when that company was taken over, made the new Island Sailing a major force.

By 1987 the company had 250 boats, and it was becoming clear that economies of scale were what would bring profits in this business. This thinking and the encouragement of financial backers led to Island taking over YCA to form Sunsail. The holding company's 640 boats was probably the biggest cruising yacht fleet in the world, and the fleet was still expanding.

In 1989, with a fall-off in demand mirroring the economy in general, Sunsail found itself disposing of boats it did not need, and there were no new purchases in the following year. With the recession foreign markets became more important; an office was opened in Munich in 1987 and a partnership was formed with a Caribbean charter organisation to market the entire Sunsail programme in North America. YCA had produced a French-language brochure back in 1978, but flotilla sailing remained a predominantly British activity. Dutch companies were appearing in Greece, and German sailors would use Sunsail, but as a provider of 'bare-boats'. By 1991 the company was leapfrogging from the Caribbean to the coast of Thailand.

An experiment with skiing holidays promptly ceased trading, but the watersports clubs were a

Marmaris Town Quay in 1982. *M. Cox*

successful venture. At the time of the merger YCA ran three residential clubs on the Mediterranean, and Island Sailing one. By 1991 there were five – two in Turkey and three in Greece – providing land-based holidays or the 'villa flotilla' option. In addition the option for individuals to own a yacht, funding it over a period through company use, continued to be attractive. The boats, in contrast to the early days when they were brought from England and builders almost had to be begged to provide them, were now largely provided by the French manufacturers, and a company like Sunsail could have a big influence on design and cost.

Like most of the other companies, YCA had become established in Yugoslavia, and in 1987 had a flotilla of Sigma 33s sailing the Dalmatian coast and Kornati Islands, together with another flotilla of Adriatic 950s. The latter were Yugoslav-owned; Eric thinks this was probably on the principle that Yugoslav boats couldn't be nationalised. Mike Cox continued in his role as Operations Director under Sunsail, and when the war broke out in Yugoslavia he hired local fishermen at very short notice to move the boats out 'with the smell of cordite in the air'. Another setback at this time was the takeover of Sunsail by AirBreak, a small public company that subsequently ceased trading. Sunsail itself was still trading successfully, and the brand was bought at very short notice from the Administrators by the venture capital investors who had already had a stake in the Sunsail business. This period in the early 1990s marks the big step in the flotilla business from small independent companies to multinationals.

# Part 2
# Some Ionian Places

# ‖
# Introduction and routes

This part of the book is not a good-food guide. Nor is it a good-drinks guide, or a good-company guide. It is certainly not a good-harbour guide or a good-village guide.

The tavernas and restaurants found in these pages are here because they are part of the general story that this book sets out to tell, with roots in the 1970s, because the original families still run them and were prepared to contribute their reminiscences, or because contributors mentioned them and provided photos.

Each of the harbours in the Ionian now has a number of places to eat. The bigger towns have a great many, as well as bars, coffee-and-snack shops and even restaurants providing specialist menus like Italian, French or Chinese food. Each year some change hands, and new ones are opened. I have eaten in some of them, but by no means all. Some wonderful restaurants that I try never to miss on a cruise are not even mentioned here, and several important towns are not represented.

Even within these criteria there are gaps. 'Chicken Billy' had died before the idea for the book was born, and his tiny place in Spartahori has been a shop and a store-room (though the plaque on the wall above the door is still there remembering him).

I have explained all this to my Greek friends whose stories are not included here. In the very early days at Nidri there were just two restaurants, and the lead-crews did their best to tell the flotilla sailors that they were equally good. I very much hope that nothing I have written here departs from this sort of even-handedness.

## North or South Ionian?

As described in earlier chapters, a small flotilla of Jaguars was established at Corfu by Greek Island Yachting Holidays for the 1976 season, and the company grew during subsequent years. YCA's flotillas arrived in 1977 and before the end of the decade there were half a dozen companies offering yacht-based and land-based sailing holidays in the Ionian. For the flotilla companies a major decision was, and still is, which town or village to use for the turn-arounds. This decision depended on which islands the flotilla aimed to visit, but also on access to the airport. Corfu airport was the only Ionian option until 1982.

Different companies made different decisions about changeover locations and about the routes for the flotillas. GIYH had begun in Corfu merely because Tom Keen's two sons were based there, but Sailing Holidays, as the company is now called, has always enjoyed the northern area and has recently developed a 'Faraway Islands' route that visits the island group to the north of Corfu: they also visit Vonitsa in the Gulf of Amvrakia behind Preveza. At the same time the company has routes that can include the Dragonera Island in the south-east or Poros on Cephalonia in the south-west, and it currently has one of its bases at Sivota as well as offering holidays from Fiscardo.

In the early years Paxos was a popular location for turn-around despite the ferry trip, even once Preveza airport became available. Plateria and

Mourtos Town Quay in 1979. *Sailing Holidays*

other mainland ports have now been developed as mainland alternatives within reach of the Southern Ionian. YCA used Levkas Town for some changeovers in 1982; subsequently almost every quay on Levkas has been used by one company or another, from Nikiana to Vasiliki, and Preveza and Paleros on the mainland are also flotilla bases. Neilson flotillas have a hotel link in Nidri, and Sunsail has a purpose-built harbour at Vounaki. Argostoli airport on Cephalonia has led to flotillas being based on that island too, though the Levkas region offers the shorter distances and sheltered harbours that lead-crews like for the start of their journeys.

Corfu and the adjacent islands already had a thriving tourist industry of its own in 1976. Towards the end of that season Mike Cox was given the task of visiting the Ionian islands to make a survey with a view to bringing YCA flotillas there. He carried a Dictaphone, and what he recorded was subsequently typed up back in Guildford. He also hand-wrote his impressions of the villages and their facilities for visiting boats, the harbours and many of the isolated bays, and produced sketches of the layout of many of the harbours, which were later reproduced in cruising notes for clients.

Mike's survey notes are quoted at length here to illustrate the way decisions about routes were made, but also to give the flavour of the region in the mid-1970s.

About Paxos, Mike says:

'It is situated in what must be one of the most attractive natural harbours in the Med. Obviously with such a fine harbour and attractive town it is very popular with yachtsmen and consequently suffers from overcrowding throughout the season.'

About Vathi on Meganisi he says:

'Ample quay space on the western side … small taverna down on the front … ladies in national dress … no natural water, but a water tap.'

These quotations sum up the reason that the locations described in this second part of the book are all southern ones. As transport links have improved most of the villages have provided some facilities for holidaymakers who don't come in yachts, but in general the southern islands don't

Sivota Bay, Levkas, in 1985. *Sailing Holidays*

have long sandy beaches. In the 'Inland Sea' between Levkas, Cephalonia and the mainland much of the change has occurred since the 1970s, and through the influence of the boats rather than because of land-based tourism.

Mike's notes begin:

'The area in general offers an excellent opportunity for flotilla sailing. The scenery and towns are interesting and varied, from the busy tourist resorts of the north to the unspoilt villages and bays of Meganisi and the "Inland Sea".

In fact the difference between North and South is quite marked not only in scenery – the South being more rugged and mountainous – but also in customs and dress. In many of the islands the women, young and old alike, still dress in colourful local costumes.

The people of Ithaca – traditionally seafarers – are more sophisticated and affluent than those of the nearby islands and most of them speak excellent Australian.

Throughout the whole area the people are friendly and helpful and really seem to enjoy the company of visitors. The scenery is magnificent in most of the area and, especially in Spring and early Summer, is really colourful. At this time of year wild flowers grow in profusion. During deliveries our budding botanist identified 24 different species of wild orchids!'

The Southern Ionian islands were known to the YCA lead-crews because they were on the route for the delivery trips between Brindisi and the Saronic Gulf. It was clearly an ideal charter area, with plenty of islands, villages and swim-stops, mainly over quite short distances. The original worry was getting the clients to the sailing area.

In those days charter planes were often delayed. There were plenty of charter flights going to Greece in the 1970s, but the regional airports we are used to today were not then available, so the new businesses depended on Athens and Corfu. People going to the Saronic Gulf had 2½-hour transfers by coach. For the Sporades the bus transfer was 4½ hours, but since the road journey was on the mainland it was always possible, however late the flight arrived.

Corfu airport was used for the early Ionian flotillas. It was Mike's view that Corfu itself was too far north to begin a cruise centred on the area they really wanted people to use, which was the Ionian Inland Sea, south of the Levkas Canal. Looking

The Ionian chart printed in the YCA brochure in 1977. YCA

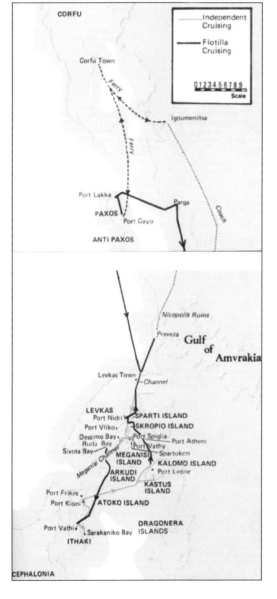

back, Mike can clearly see how the decision was made to use this route in 1977:

> 'It was all two-week cruises in those days but the leg from Corfu to Parga is 30 miles and from Parga to Levkas is 35 miles – each a full day's sailing. Fine going south, but when you're going north with a good north-wester it's a beat all the way, and hard work. Doing this twice within the fortnight would have been too much, especially as when returning you had to get there to catch the flight.'

The first YCA flotilla customers were either taken from Corfu on a ferry to Paxos or to Igoumenitsa, then an hour and a half on a coach to Preveza. Mike says:

> 'It was a real nightmare if you got people stuck on Corfu island. I think in the first year we had two or maybe three occasions when we had to overnight people in Corfu because their flight was so late that there were no ferries to bring them south.'

There was a company called Greek Sail who started about the same time in the Ionian and eventually became Island Sailing in about '78 or '79. They had the same worry. They tried operating out of Corfu in their first year. People were worn out – they had to get down and back.'

Mike goes on:

> 'We open-jawed to give a bigger area. ['Open-jawed' is a charter term meaning that the cruise starts and finishes at different ends of the route.] One group would start at Paxos and finish at Preveza. Then the next group would start at Preveza and finish at Paxos. It saved them having to do the long journey twice. Later on we sometimes used Paleros instead of Preveza.
>
> From Port Gaios on Paxos we usually went to Lakka on the first day. A short trip on the first day is still important for two main reasons. First, the Greek paperwork has to be done, and that can't be completed until the people have arrived. In those days there was a

mountain of documentation because there wasn't a separate law to cover chartering so all the boats were treated separately as merchant ships – a nightmare for the lead-crews. Second, a short trip gave the staff a chance to look at all the different people to make sure they were capable of handling the boats, and if they weren't maybe someone would be put on board to give them a hand.'

Right from the start clients who hadn't much experience in handling a boat were catered for; YCA used to say if someone came on a two-day course on the Solent with them they would know enough to take a boat on a flotilla.

On the following day the boats would go to Parga on the mainland, a sail of fifteen or twenty miles. Often this would become a two-day stop depending on the weather; the sailors might enjoy a day on the beach there, or go out for a day-sail. Then the following day would be the long haul south.

It wasn't difficult going south because the wind was almost invariably from astern, but the boats had to stick together because of the difficulty of identifying the entrance to the Levkas Canal.

'In those days there was no question of stopping at Levkas because all the sewers emptied into the canal so the group of boats motored through and went to Nidri.'

Once at Nidri the route would sometimes go as far west as Fiscardo, or as far east as Paleros (then called Zaverda), but centred on Meganisi, the east coast of Ithaca and sometimes Kalamos. Ayios Andreas was visited too, a beautiful bay in the south of Ithaca with space for only a few boats owing to the depth, so nowadays rarely visited other than by private boats. The tradition of holding barbecues began in the Sporades because there were so few different places to eat. They proved very popular, and in the Ionian Abeliki Bay was used. The journey continued via Nidri to Preveza, and the next flotilla would begin from there.

This is marvellous isn't it girls?

Yes John, but does it have to lean over this far?

*Barrie Neilson*

# 12
# Levkas

## Sivota

Sivota used to be difficult to spot from a distance – Rod Heikell says so as late as 1992 in the first edition of his Ionian sailing guide. Ernle Bradford, who visited Levkas more than thirty years earlier than that, makes no reference to this bay, though in his *Companion Guide to the Greek Islands* he writes about many smaller anchorages and clearly loves isolated and beautiful places.

The recently built villas on the hillside near the mouth of the bay make the entrance much easier to spot now, and steady development of the quayside and village has made this a much-visited harbour.

Of all the locations in the Ionian this is the one whose original character early visitors guard most jealously in their memory. The natural beauty of the hills and the shelter of the harbour remain; those of us who got to know Sivota more recently would be poor observers if we just regarded it as a

Entering Sivota Bay, 1977. *YCA*

*H*ammond Innes, 1965: 'Levkas port is no more than a quay facing the first bend of the canal... There are no other ports of consequence in Levkas, and the three anchorages we visited – Vasilico, Sivota and Vliko – are much as Odysseus must have know them... Skropio [sic] ... had a road bulldozed round it. We thought at first it must be an oil company setting up a drilling rig. We later discovered that ... Onassis was developing the whole island as a gambling centre.

Sivota ... is entirely different – no village here, just three farmsteads at the head of a dog-legged gut in the rocky coast... The atmosphere ... is entirely pastoral. It is as though three nomadic families have settled in a place of supreme beauty.'

sheltered spot with a quay that can take plenty of boats and has lots of good places to eat and drink. During the winter of 1975 Mike Cox was leading a YCA delivery crew, bringing the first group of Mirage 28s from Brindisi to the Saronic gulf. They used the bay for overnight shelter and can claim to have enjoyed the first meal in the Ionian to be served to sailors on flotilla boats. Mike's team rowed ashore, and asked at the only cafe if it would be possible to get anything to eat. Two chickens were brought out and weighed, their necks were wrung and they were served up three hours later; meanwhile, Mike and his crew were served with copious quantities of retsina.

At that stage there were no tavernas at Sivota, but the first two were soon in place; Panayotis developed and extended his café, which is now run by his daughter Spiradoula and called No Problem, and Spiros opened his place, the Delfinia, where his son Yannis is now the guiding force. Spiros's brother Stavros soon set up his own establishment – the family name Fatouros is everywhere in this village.

When Mike made his survey for YCA in 1976 to prepare for the flotillas, he wrote:

'Just along the coast is Sivota, which has total shelter and a magnificent setting. A very poor hamlet lies along the shore here consisting of no more than a dozen houses. They are as yet without electricity and seem to be just entering the twentieth century. A total feeling of calm and tranquillity prevails and for a quiet night afloat it would be difficult to think of anywhere better. Ashore there is a small café which has very limited stock; however, if any fish has been caught by the locals that day they will willingly cook it for you. A freshwater spring provides all the village's drinking water and a drink from here is delicious after walking up the valley behind Sivota to enjoy the view. To discover an anchorage like Sivota must be every cruising man's dream.'

After YCA began its flotillas in the area it used Sivota to moor its boats over the winter and work on them. Later Sunsail had a flotilla base here, and now Sailing Holidays has an office. However, the quay was only started in the 1980s. The first section was part of the long side of the bay towards the entrance to the harbour, and the rest was built bit by bit, finishing in 1990 with the section that curves round at the head of the bay. Boats moored off, at one point on permanent moorings, and the crews came ashore by dinghy.

In 1982 an article about flotilla sailing in *Yachting World* called Sivota 'a superbly sheltered circular natural harbour almost untouched by progress'.

The original buildings are spread right round the present quay. The road and most of the space used for restaurant tables stands on the in-filled area, which brought the quay out into deep enough water for yachts, and the old buildings are incorporated in the back of the present ones or even free-standing behind a new structure. Amongst the original buildings are two at the head of the harbour, a number at the side of the bay including No Problem, the Old Store and Yanna's Family Restaurant, a group at the back of the Delfinia restaurant, and the bar at the harbour-mouth end of the road.

In those days water came from a single well and was very difficult to get for visiting boats. There was no question of power – electricity had arrived, but not all round the bay. Now of course shore-power for boats is available all round the dock. The

**D**oug Kennett came here with his family in 1976: 'A conspicuous white hut standing alone on the shore aided entry to the bay, and one anchored in splendid isolation in 3-8 metres over mud and weed, as there was no quay. This beautiful, tranquil haven was unoccupied except for a few families. I hope my poem conveys the tranquillity of Greece in those days.'

## Early Morning in Sivota Bay

As I lie in my bunk I hear seconds tick by,
And I gaze through the hatch to a starry sky
That gazes back on the now silent sea,
On the bay, on the village, on the owls and on
  me.

Our now silent ship in the near silent bay
Will soon come alive with the noise of the day,

But the cocks that now to each other do crow
Will quieten themselves when the sun starts to
  grow.

The sun will soon raise each man and his wife
Who will work in the hills, as is their life,
And donkeys and goats and sheep I'll see
Climbing up through the hills away from the sea.

The raucous bray of the laden beast,
And the wind brought about by the fire in the
  east,
And the urgent noise of our children at play
Will change this still scene of our ship in the bay.

But now a few moments of silence I'll sip
With the owls and the stars and our little ship;
Before this dual scene is made one by the wind
I'll also reflect – both in sea and in mind.

*Sivota Bay, Greece, 0500 hours, 4 May 1976*

Doug Kennett sailed his yacht *Ndoto* from the UK to the Mediterranean with his young family in 1976: here they are moored in isolation in Sivota Bay. *Doug Kennett*

*Above* Sivota in the 1980s: no road or new quay yet. *YCA*

*Below* Before the quay was built only two or three boats could moor alongside.
Here two flotillas are moored off in quiet weather. *Ian Meikle*

one telephone in the village was at Panayotis's taverna, supplied by the port police. From the early flotilla days there were two tavernas here; now there are seven big restaurants, shops, bars and cafés, and the harbour is quite rarely less than full by the evening.

**Yannis from the Delfinia restaurant** is one of those who remembers the overwintering in the early days. Like everyone else who lived here then, his family earned their living from fishing and growing olives. You only need to see him moving

about his fishing-boat to know that he is a born seaman and, like all farmers, he has a constant eye on the weather: 'We have water on this island, 150 metres down. The olives need rain though, and we have had dry winters.'

'They put mooring rings in the corner, and in the spring brought the boats up on the beach for antifouling. [This was on the little beach where small boats are still launched, in the corner of the bay nearest to the entrance.] There was no quay, just a small wooden jetty

Scott Brown was a YCA skipper in 1983. He says his most memorable time was 'lounging with Tassos at the Captain's Cabin in Fiscardo', but he also sent this photo of Yannis at Sivota treading olives. Scott also says, 'I remember Paniotis from the "No Problem" taking us to a wedding party in the hills, of one of his relatives. Being the guest of honour (well, it was the third day of the party – they were running out of

celebrities), I had to dance with the oldest lady while everyone clapped - a handkerchief dance with a 4ft 10in 90-year-old. At 6ft 1in it was a touch difficult when I was supposed to go under her arm. I have no photos of that night, which surprises me as my engineer lived on the story of my dancing for some time.' *Scott Brown*

*Above* 'Early morning in Sivota Bay in 1978': from a YCA brochure, showing the Delfinia restaurant. *Eric Richardson*

*Below* The buildings shown in the above photo as they are in 2007, seen at the back of the restaurant – the house furthest from the camera is the restaurant's kitchen. *Author*

*Above* This picture, reproduced by kind permission of
Spiradoula at the No Problem taverna, shows the
building around which the restaurant was built; today
it is behind the stairway, which now gives access to
the first floor of the modern building. *Author*

*Below* The restaurant in 1983. *Gordon Sharp*

*Above* Sivota Quay in 1980, with boats moored near the Delfinia. *Bill Melville*

*Below* Sivota Quay in 1983. The tower of the No Problem can be seen near the centre of the picture, and the Delfinia on the far left. *Gordon Sharp*

here. My place only had fifty chairs; there were not so many boats and on those smaller boats there were often just couples. The restaurant has only been like this for about six years: The kitchen was always at the back but the rest at the front is much bigger; it has developed gradually – it has been like this only about six years.'

As well as the people from the boats, holidaymakers come from other parts of Levkas to eat and enjoy the town at lunchtime or in the evening.

'There are more fishing-boats here now, but small ones. Thirty years ago red snapper would be 20 drachma a kilo – nothing! There are lots less fish now. There are laws, but some fish like whitebait don't grow big, so a little net for that fish catches the bigger ones as well. And the big boats, maybe from Patras, pull their nets for five or six hours and kill everything.'

Every day, like everyone else in Sivota, Yannis sees the new buildings on the hillsides. Everyone hopes the government regulations requiring 4,000

One of the houses at the head of the quay in 1983 and the same house
once the quay had been extended. *Gordon Sharp/Kevan Dearman*

square metres of open land around a private building outside the village will be enough to avoid the 'hill becoming a city'. However, you don't have to be a surveyor as you sail into Sivota to wonder where the open land is around some of the buildings.

Yannis points out a house opposite with no balcony and a very non-traditional shape: 'Look at that one! Like a jail!' Nevertheless he is confident that Sivota could never become like Nidri, if only for lack of space. He says few of the houses belong to Greeks: there are Italians, British, Dutch. But development has brought work and prosperity: 'We start with nothing here.'

Yannis gets on with all the skippers but says, 'Now they just come for one year, for fun. In the old days we saw them year after year – they would come in wet from their dinghies!'

The first part of the quay was built in 1982, but still only two or three boats could be on it, and the others rafted or moored off.

**Yannis from the Ionian restaurant** says:

'I believe the flotillas were a good idea to let people learn about sailing like a sailing school, and I see people who come with their families and every day they learn a bit more about where to go and what to do. At the same time all the group is together and the skippers know what to do and can give information about the history and about what to do. People get experience and after a few years maybe they start to come on their own.'

Yannis points out that a lot of the development that has happened over the last years was due to flotillas, as it was one of the first ways people could come here.

'Originally a lot of the hotels and rooms in the Ionian were low quality and in small numbers, but because of the flotillas a lot of people came to isolated islands. In the islands a lot of people had no jobs and they were moving to the big cities. That's why Athens grew so big, but now that trend has stopped and people are able to come back to their place of birth and work in tourism, either directly or indirectly.

Plenty of families away from the harbours can make their living too.'

Like everyone in Sivota he thinks of the harbour as a practical workplace.

'We still have some difficulties over yachts mooring where the fishermen work. The fishermen try to do their job, and often their boats are old and fragile; maybe some sailors are not so experienced in mooring or anchoring properly. Also the fishermen pile their nets on the quay and sometimes yachts come and moor there so it is not easy for them. Some of the fishermen are old and they don't speak English – everyone is doing their job and has to try to cooperate.

Most of the houses on the hillside are villas to rent. A lot of visitors now want more than a simple kitchen and bathroom – a pool and jacuzzi, and isolation. There are now more buildings outside than in the village itself. Like in England it is hard for local people to afford houses. Some of the fields where the villas were built were just bushes, no olive trees, so were sold very cheap originally, but now it is more expensive up there – some who sold their land later on made a lot of money.'

Yannis continues:

'The Ionian Restaurant started in 1982, just here but two levels higher, because back then the sea was here. There was a nice veranda, steps up, access was through the yards you see on the side, but in 1990 when they made the road the restaurant could be much deeper. That's what happened along the whole of the quay – the restaurants stayed in the same place with extended yards in front.'

Janet Welch first came to Sivota in the early 1980s and writes that she still visits Nikos (Yannis's father) 'and his charming family. We used to sit on the quay and have a drink with Grandfather Fatouros (Nick's father). He could not speak English and our Greek is very limited. But he was a lovely chap!'

# Vasiliki

Mike Cox's survey notes said:

'The village is situated in the NE corner of a large bay with high mountains all round. The quay is well sheltered and in good condition. It is suitable for alongside or bows-to mooring. The downdrafts that Denham speaks of would perhaps be a little uncomfortable but there is no fetch for the sea and I don't foresee it being a problem. Ashore there are a few simple shops and quite a pleasant taverna situated right on the quay. Water is also obtainable on the quay.'

**Hammond Innes:** 'Vasilico: There are three protected anchorages here. The outer has a good depth and the protection of a broken mole now partly awash. The second is sheltered by a solid quay and is the waterfront of the fishing village. The third is right against the sandy shore, the arms of the breakwaters almost entirely submerged … clearly it belonged to the days of ancient Greece when craft were small and invariably dragged up the beach… In the heat of the day the waterfront of this little fishing village sleeps under the shade of its plane trees.'

Vasiliki in 1980: sweeping up while olives are being pressed. *Bill Melville*

Two more views of Vasiliki in 1980: bringing in the catch at the main harbour. *Both Bill Melville*

## Nidri

Nidri was very different in the 1970s. The whole of what is now the main quay, the road in front of it, and most of the outdoor parts of the restaurants are infill, created and improved over the intervening years. There were only two restaurants anyway, and they were at the line of the present buildings. In front of them were perhaps a couple of small tables and a rough track, then the water. There was a small quay there that the flotillas used, next to the old ferry quay, and a private jetty that belonged to Aristotle Onassis who used it for access to Scorpios. Quite often yachts would moor in Tranquil Bay.

The present road to Sivota was just a track through the mountains. There were two tavernas. One belonged to Nick the Greek, who was a friend of Onassis and who went out in a fishing-boat with Mike Cox to help with the survey of Meganisi. The other belonged to Gregory, and of course there was constant rivalry between them. The flotilla leaders just had to say that each was as good as the other. Within a year there were two or three more tavernas – and so on!

In 1976 one of Mike Cox's concerns was not only to suggest places suitable for overnight stops, but to find a possible location for a changeover base. He rejected Levkas largely because of the 'offensive' smell from the surrounding lagoons and mudflats (this sewage problem was to be improved within a few years), but also because of lack of free space on the quay.

*L*awrence **Durrell:** 'If you set out from Nydri, a pretty little port, you will have to skirt a number of small islets which confuse perspectives and outlines, and will find yourself wondering how on earth the mariners of old ever managed to operate before the first maps were available.'

**Hammond Innes on Vliko:** 'You sail past old villas big as English country houses. Mud flats to starboard, a small village, then you are in the narrows. At the narrowest point there is a boatyard full of caiques hauled out for repair. When we anchored there the people were coming in from the fields, ponies, donkeys, women and even men laden with the coarse verdure they use for fodder. There was a well tap close by the kaffeneion and women passed in endless procession with pots of water balanced on their heads.'

'Nidri offers an excellent alternative to Levkas as a stop. The village is fast expanding into a tourist resort (although it is a long way behind the established ones). Many boats now ply out of here to the surrounding bays and islands, and a small quay is in the process of being enlarged and the bottom dredged… The locals are very tourist-conscious and hotels and tavernas are springing up all along the front. All provisions are obtainable and fresh bread is baked almost on the quay itself.'

Nidri street in 1984. Not just a quiet day – all days were quieter then. *Gordon Sharp*

# 13
# Meganisi

Mike Cox's planning notes for YCA in 1976 say: 'The island, pleasantly located in the shelter of Levkas, is a veritable treasure trove of bays and beaches.' Mike was shown round this area in a motorboat by 'Nick the Greek' who ran (and still runs) a taverna at Nidri. Like the Denham pilot book, he begins with Port Atheni, describing a good sheltered anchorage and a 30-minute walk through olive groves to Vathahori, from where there is a good view of Ithaca and the southern islands. He spots the potential of Abeliki Bay for barbecues.

Meganisi is a beautiful and still unspoiled island, but it is now hovering on the edge of major development. Its position close to Nidri makes it accessible for day-trippers, but if ever there was a place whose main attraction is to the yachtsman this is it: the many sheltered inlets provide swimming anchorages everywhere, but there are few natural areas of flat land at water level and no extensive beaches. The beauty of the hillsides, still largely given over to olive trees and goats, is best seen from the deck of a boat, and the wonderful villages are just far enough away from the harbours to provide an early-evening stroll.

However, the breathtaking views from almost every olive grove and in almost any direction have led to the building of an increasing number of villas for holidaymakers on the hillsides. Some are in keeping with the locality. Some, like the hotel that faces towards Nidri, are, in the polite words of a taverna-owner, 'not very pretty'. The local mayors have useful powers to control building outside the limits of villages. Meganisi has already become rich: a local man described it as the Mykanos of the Ionian, explaining that he meant in terms of prosperity not style, but let's hope the council keeps it that way.

Hammond Innes visited Meganisi in the mid-1960s. He moored in Port Atheni and walked up to the village:

'Of all the islands of the Ionian, Meganisi was the one we loved the best. Here you are back in the Middle Ages, the streets rough stony tracks … on Sunday evening … the whole village was out of doors … the women in traditional costume … the men with their usual courtesy made room for us on the veranda of the kaffeneion. Out of kindness to visitors from the sea the proprietor cooked us some fish "borrowed" from a village family, whilst his small son did a roaring trade in the brochettes that they call solaiki – little skewers of mutton grilled then sprinkled with rough sea salt mixed with oregano, finally a squeeze of lemon… The top restaurants of the world would be hard put to it to produce meat more delectable.'

## Porto Spiglia

The flotillas that first came to Porto Spiglia were attracted by the lovely village of Spartahori. As now, the visitors walked up the steep path to the village. Mooring was on the long concrete quay, where the fishing-boats went too. The seabed shelves very steeply here; in effect you dropped your anchor and as much line as possible into a deep hole, and hauled it up until it dug into something.

Early visitors to the village from flotilla boats fondly remember Chicken Billy's taverna with just half a dozen small tables, up in the heart of the village, and enjoying his omelettes and his hospitality. Billy the Chicken died some years ago, and there is only the little plaque above the door to remind passers-by of the cave-like bottle-lined room that opened onto the street, where visitors and the old men of the village were made to feel equally at home, with newspaper cuttings and poems pinned on the wall remembering the days when Aristotle and Christina Onassis used to visit.

Porto Spiglia Taverna is the biggest taverna in the Ionian. Today Babis or one of the waiters will help you moor, and Panos will appear in his rubber boat to bring your boat in when there is rough weather, or will dive for your anchor if you lose it in the murky depths.

In 1982 their father and mother had a small barbecue at the foot of the road up to the village. Babis says that his father built the original place from the local stone; he used to have a small supermarket in the village and a caique that operated to and from the mainland before there was a ferry. But his family also owned land by the harbour, and it is there that the present business has grown up.

The original building had a bamboo roof and forty chairs. It was a family business; a visitor remembers the ten-year-old Babis snoozing in a chair and being nudged awake when a group from one of the (maybe) ten yachts came ashore.

Babis says:

'Flotillas were a good idea. Most people would not have come here alone. Around 1978 we saw the first flotillas: YCA, Seascape, the Baby Bens. Maybe there would be twenty-five boats between all the ports here. They anchored here in the bay.'

The family built a small wooden jetty in front of the taverna, and in the mid-1990s built and then extended their floating pontoon, with lazy-lines. Later the main stone quay was extended, providing an inner basin for fishing-boats and allowing visiting boats to use most of the original quay as far as the ferry berth. Anchoring was still a problem on the old quay because of the depth of water, and now the family have installed lazy-lines there too.

A vigorous development like this has inevitably brought some controversy. Visiting yachts whose crews moor on the taverna's own pontoon and eat their meal on board presumably don't realise that this is not just another village-owned quay and that it might be polite to have a drink at least with the people whose waiters took their lines. The rivalry that existed with the next-door Asteria taverna could be uncomfortable for those who didn't eat there, but had to walk past. Moreover, the installation of lazy-lines on the town quay seemed to the villagers at first like a land-grab; it is to be

Mike Cox surveyed the Ionian for YCA in late 1976, and immediately spotted the potential of Meganisi as a cruising ground. The section of his notes reproduced here includes the brief reference to Spiglia: 'one or two yachts could lie bows to...'. *YCA*

BILLY THE CHICKEN

SPARTOHORI

MEGANISI – LEFKAS

TEL. (0645) 51-442

*Ian Meikle*

*Left* Billy in 1995. *Author*

*Below* Billy's taverna in the 1990s: boxes of wine bottles stacked on the floor and extra chairs ready to be set out in the street. *Author*

*Above* Mooring at Porto Spiglia in 1980: a flotilla is double-moored, but most of the quay is taken up with local boats. Neither the ferry landing nor the short protective quay beyond it had been built at that time. *Bill Melville*

*Below* In 1981 the area near the harbour at Porto Spiglia showed signs of the development to come later, but the route from yachts moored at the old quay to the bottom of the steep footpath leading to the village was still largely given over to olive trees and fishermen's nets. *John Hooker*

Porto Spiglia in 1983: the road around the headland was not there till much later, of course. The ferry landing was then very new and the quay beyond it had not been built. Yachts could find a space between the ferry and fishing-boats, though anchoring there required a great deal of warp and chain. Nowadays boats can be moored at the old quay, the adjacent new stone quay or the floating pontoons nearby, or at the newer jetty at the head of the bay by the beach. All these berths have lazy-lines. *Ian Meikle*

hoped that everyone now realises that the ability to moor 120 boats securely and to avoid crossed anchors brings boats and business to everyone. No longer is it necessary to help five or six boats untangle themselves every day. In the early days it was just Mr and Mrs Konidaris doing the cooking. In 2006 the Asteria Taverna was rented to the Porta Spiglia Taverna and run as part of the bigger business; there are 650 chairs and thirty-five people work there in the summer.

Babis is proud that mooring is safer now.

'It is important to have nice waiters, good staff. We work hard. I give my blood for my business. Sometimes we stay up all night in bad weather to look after the boats on the jetty … me two hours, Panos two hours, one of the others two hours. We have customers who have been coming for twenty years.'

## Vathi

Even in the early 1990s yachts could only moor on the right-hand side of the harbour – the part of the quay at the far end was too shallow. The town has always seemed what it is: a real village with a life and population of its own. The development of the town square included a small playground for children, and sometimes a 'local derby' basketball match can be seen on the court there, perhaps between the boys of Vathi and Spartahori.

The older houses round the harbour have gradually been renovated, and are now being joined by new buildings, some of them villas for summer rental. This building and the extended mooring around the bay signal considerable growth for this charming town. Like everywhere else in the area the people hope the essence of the place doesn't change, while welcoming further opportunities for local employment.

A few years ago a new taverna with lazy-lines for about twenty-five boats was opened in an inlet towards the mouth of the bay. During 2007 a new quay was built on the left-hand side of the harbour, opposite most of the buildings, with a floating breakwater. In 2008 work started in the inlet next to the church on what is planned to be a marina, though local opinion is divided on whether it will be for visiting boats or whether smaller boats and fishing-boats will use it, allowing the main harbour to be modified for further yachts. What is clear is that the capacity of the village to receive yachts is doubling and redoubling. Water and power are now available on the quays from token-operated machines.

The Rose Garden Taverna has a sign reading

1983 and 2007 views, looking from the harbour towards the inlet where
the new marina is planned. *Gordon Sharp/Bernard Jakeways*

'1969' over the door – originally Stefanos's family had a small supermarket. In the early days the taverna would serve whatever it had at the time or could buy: chicken fried in olive oil, pork chops in the oven, a small souvlaki. Effie, Stefanos's daughter, says:

> 'Slowly we learned other dishes – maybe just adding mousaka, cooked tomatoes. The produce came from Levkas; there was no ferry then, just a boat that left at 6.30am. The journey took 2½ hours; you would do the shopping and get back here at 4.00pm. It was easy to offer fish as there were plenty here. The only milk we could get was tinned milk. At the start there might be one flotilla a week. When we were the only place here twenty or twenty-five people seemed like a hundred. Now we have the tables across the road and can seat 150 people, but the square was only opened in 1988.'

Until 1988 the square was closed off by a fence; this was to protect the trees, which were newly planted there, from animals. The ferry started because of tourism. A small one started in May 1984 and used to go to Levkas, while the bigger one to Nidri came later; in the 1970s Nidri was by no means the local centre it is now, with a fast road to Levkas, but just a few houses; people came to Vathi to sell lemons and oranges, and the Vathi fishermen sold at a market over there.

Effie's brother Stathis says tourism has been good and bad.

> 'The place has kept its identity, and could never change as much as Nidri has. Meganisi is quite rich now; in the past all the families depended on fishing, or else they went to Athens to find work, or emigrated. There are fewer fish, but there is still a big fishing-boat here. Now there is work here for young people, and each year people come back from Athens. In the first years the people who cooked food did it not just for the money, but because it was the Greek way – hospitality. It happened at first from inside – an offer, not a job. Visitors asked what you had – if you cooked an egg that was everything. Amongst the older people there used to be the traditional way of life, and everyone would dance very readily. That generation has nearly gone now.'

Erricos's Porto Vathi restaurant near the ferry quay opened in 1978, at first specialising in fish. Erricos comes from a fishing family, and says that his father used to buy just boxes of fish on the quay, though now the menu offers a full range including meat and pasta. His restaurant is well-positioned to benefit from the new moorings planned for the cove by the church but, while he relishes the idea of eighty yacht spaces there, he insists, like others in the village, that development must be for the benefit of local people.

In 2007 the harbour is almost full. The new moorings on both sides of the entrance are not shown in this view. *Author*

*Above* This 1983 view shows the buildings beyond the harbour, with the jetty in the foreground. *Gordon Sharp*

*Below* The 2007 equivalent also shows the buildings, but is taken from the foot of the jetty because of the awnings of Erricos's restaurant. The jetty itself was rebuilt and extended in 2008. *Author*

Work under way in 2008 on the new marina. *Author*

Once dredging had begun the new area was being used for mooring at the same time as construction work went on. *Author*

*Below* The floating crane at work at the seaward side of the inlet destined to be the new marina. *Author*

# 14
# Ithaca

## Vathi

Mike Cox has a long section on Vathi in the notes he made on his survey for YCA in 1976. As well as the town itself, he writes about the village of Palaiochora on the saddle behind the town, and of the possible walk to Sarakiniko Cove on the east side of the island, which he says has good shelter and offers an excellent alternative to Vathi for those who don't mind the two-mile walk into the town. Together with other small coves on that side of Ithaca, which he describes as only really suitable for day stops, he points out that the main ferry route passes close by and this creates a large swell that could be dangerous – boats must be warned not to anchor too close to the beach. It is interesting that this possible hazard is nowadays largely mentioned in relation to Frikes, where even with the modern harbour it is necessary to moor in an area sheltered from the ferry-wash. Early pilot books speak similarly of Kioni, but the extended mole and quay have considerably modified the shelter there.

Of the town itself, Mike says:

'Vathi is set in magnificent surroundings at the head of a long and interesting bay. Unfortunately it is slightly marred as a port by the strong winds that funnel down the bay in the afternoons and evenings. The harbour is sheltered but too small for a fleet [here he is speaking of the inner basin now dedicated to local fishing or tripper boats] and it would be necessary to anchor off in the areas indicated on the harbour plan. The town itself has everything we could need for a flotilla stop although water is difficult and a little expensive. (During the deliveries we paid 50 drachmas per boat for a water-truck to come.) Most of the town is relatively modern due to the earthquake, of which much can still be seen in the way of ruined buildings. The waterfront has ample cafés and tavernas, gift shops, etc, and it is not difficult to imagine that you're in Melbourne or Sydney when the locals talk to you. The mythology of the island is very much alive and adds to the interest of the town and island.'

**Lawrence Durrell:** 'The entry to Vathi harbour will set the atmosphere for a first visit – it is remarkable as well as beautiful. The bare stone sinus curves round and round – it is like travelling down the canal of the inner ear of a giant. One is seized with a sense of vertigo: will the harbour never come in sight? It does at last, buried at the very end of this stony lobe of rock.'

**Ernle Bradford:** 'The town of Vathi, which spreads in a crescent shape along all the southern shore is – despite the recent earthquake – a pleasant place in which to find oneself. The cleanliness of its narrow alleys would put many a modern city to shame, and the whitewashed houses shine as clean and brilliant as the wakes of the fishing boats. Olive-oil and wine are about the only exports of the island, but most of the men are fishermen and every small bar can produce a little fresh fish to complement the wine and the ouzo.'

Mike Cox's sketch of Vathi harbour as part of his survey in 1976. *YCA*

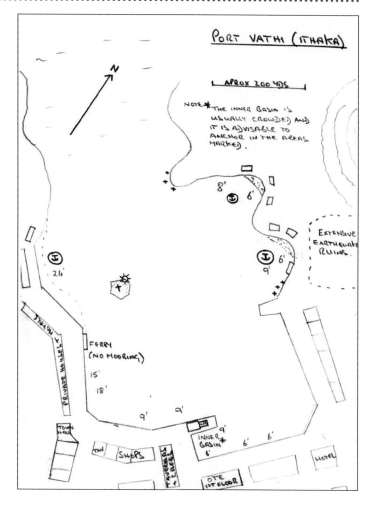

PORT VATHI (ITHAKA)

APROX 200 YDS

NOTE* THE INNER BASIN IS USUALLY CROWDED AND IT IS ADVISABLE TO ANCHOR IN THE AREAS MARKED.

EXTENSIVE EARTHQUAKE RUINS.

FERRY (NO MOORING)

PRIVATE HOUSES

SHOPS

INNER BASIN

OTE 1ST FLOOR

HOTEL

Vathi was on the early flotilla routes, but this would probably be the first time the crews had experienced serious winds – the downdraughts from the northern shore in the Gulf of Molo. Early YCA clients remember the slogan 'Mind the dandruffs!'. Originally there was nowhere much to eat in the town in the evening, though things were different at lunchtime. Visitors went to a taverna by the 'bathing' beach in the north-east corner, though the boats would often moor in town overnight in order to take advantage of shallower water and the quay. They kept well away from the ferry-boat quay in town, though, following an incident when a ferry misjudged its mooring run. The propeller-guard on the ferry 'took the top off' the Mirage 28. There was a girl in the shower at the time, who came running naked and screaming out of the boat and down the road, followed by other flotilla members with a towel.

Nowadays it is possible to moor either on the town quay at the far side from the harbour entrance, along the wall on the south-west side, to moor off in the middle of the harbour, or to turn to port as you enter the bowl of the harbour and moor to the big concrete quay that was built there relatively recently.

The Tsiribis Restaurant is one of the places to eat in this corner of the town, run by Dimitris, now working with his energetic daughter Lula, whose education in the UK enables her to take orders in English while arguing over her shoulder in Greek.

Dimitris's father bought the land and started the taverna in the early 1950s; the olive tree was there then of course, and little else but a small wooden hut. As time went on Mr Molfesis improved the road and brought in the first electrical supply to this corner, together with the first telephone.

'GW' wrote this piece for a holiday magazine in the early 1990s:

# Kalimarises!

'Sailing into Vathi, the capital of Ithaca, is a little like approaching Falmouth on a beautiful summer's day, except that the mountains are higher, there are no buildings in sight except a tiny chapel on a headland, and no other boats either except a couple of cruisers moored in a cove in the distance. This is the gulf of Aetou, and the pilot book speaks of strong gusts of wind, but we've never experienced them there. The approach takes about an hour from the time the engine is started as the mouth of the gulf is reached. In the distance behind us in the heat haze there might be a ferry from Italy moving towards the mainland. Coming from the north we skirt a headland and hear the cicadas briefly before moving out across the gulf: Odysseus's capital lies beneath the mountain ahead, but the entrance is invisible until the last moment, when it is possible to see the almost circular harbour through its narrow entrance.

We are heading for a small jetty immediately inside the harbour, opposite the small town, and right next to a taverna. Golden moments in the holiday include the first arrival here. (We shall be back next week, or the week after.) We glow

with the comfortable feeling that follows a properly judged mooring. The sails are stowed: they can be tidied later. Sweat-stained hats are thrown in the cockpit, and relatively clean tee-shirts found to add a degree of formality. The person who jumped ashore with the ropes probably stays there; the rest of us climb down and walk the twenty yards to where Dimitris is clearing the last of the lunch tables.

"Welcome home!" he says. There will be time later to hear about the rest of the family; meanwhile Dimitris brings us beers and lopes off for his afternoon sleep, leaving the door open so we can help ourselves during the afternoon. We shall swim, sit in the shade of the big olive tree, persuade ourselves we don't need to walk into town until much later, open another cold Amstel beer, regret getting a soft drink because it attracts the wasps, dodge little boys on mopeds when going back to the boat for a book, decide to swim again instead of reading.

Later on one of the waitresses will arrive and start to tidy the chairs ready for the evening. She will say "Hello" shyly, and we shall speak to her in English to emphasise how cosmopolitan she is becoming, and she will nod and smile politely and pretend to understand. Mrs Molfesis will leave the kitchen to look after itself and come to sit in the window, looking out over the tables and the harbour. We shall reach up to shake her

Entering Vathi harbour. *GW*

hand, and she will say "Kala" to indicate that her back is not too bad and she is pleased we are here, and we shall say "Kala" to mean the year has been OK and we are very happy to be back. Maybe we shall all wave our hands in front of our faces to agree how hot it is this year.

Dimitris will emerge again eventually in a clean shirt and floppy trousers, and perfect his imitation of being busy; to bustle once round the taverna carrying an order-pad, loudly humming the Pink Panther tune, before gravitating to his own chair at the high end of the taverna where his cigarette is still alight and his glass of Scottish Tea (whisky and a lot of water) is never empty.

Towards the end of the evening, when we've resolved difficult issues like how many portions of squid we should have, or which day we should be back because then Mrs Molfesis will have prepared her butter beans dish (Gigantes: oven baked in tomato and herbs, available in many places but nowhere as good as here), Dimitris will send over a tray of Metaxa, which is the sign to join him at his table and meet his friends.

Ithaca is becoming more prosperous, not least because men who left in the fifties after the earthquake and to avoid the poverty of isolation are returning to renovate their family homes following successful careers elsewhere in Europe. One year we met an Ithacan dentist from North London who discussed the West End theatre much more eruditely than we could manage, regretted the poor nutritional habits of his fellow islanders' children and feared future colonisation by junk-food chains. He insisted we visit his high-ceilinged and darkly furnished home, hung with photos and paintings of his parents and full of books. Once we had a conversation with a man called Xenophon, who asked from under hooded eyes, "Do you like Germans?" The next half-hour, which remained on a theoretical rather than personal level, acted as a reminder of Balkan tensions within the EEC. The name of the restaurant (we should give it the preferred title having eaten there) is taken from Mr Molfesis's radio call-sign when reporting ship movements to the Royal Navy during the war. Most years we discuss the marina, which is about to be built with a European grant. Luckily progress is slow; a dozen concrete blocks were placed in the harbour five years ago, which subsequently sank through the sand to just below water level, and the old men say they knew it would turn out like that. Dimitris foresees a future lording it in a holiday hot-spot surrounded by beautiful young women spending Euros like water, but irony is his strong suit even when taking an order for fish soup. His usual greeting is "Kalamarises", because he enjoys the idea that English people don't know the difference between "Good morning!" and "Squid!"

The north-east corner of Vathi harbour in 2005. The beach on the extreme left is as it must have been in the 1970s, with small bushes growing down to the water amidst large and small rocks. In the centre of the picture is the large concrete quay built in 2001, with the Tsiribis Restaurant behind it. Gregory's restaurant is amongst the trees in the foreground. In the 1970s flotillas moored off in this corner. Later some boats were able to tie up to the small concrete ferry quay, roughly where the port police storage hut is now a blot on the landscape, or to some short-lived wooden pontoons.
*Bernard Jakeways*

Dimitris in 1983. *Dimitris Molfesis*

The Tsiribis Restaurant in the early 1980s (*below*) and in 2006 (*right*). The earlier photo shows a busy day with largely local diners. In the later one the tables have been laid for the evening meal but the customers are still in their boats! The big olive tree is still there, but pruned back to allow for the new roof. *Dimitris Molfesis/GW*

The stones were broken by hand to make a floor and walls to sit on – big stones were the tables!

Of course, the population of Ithaca was 11,000 then – there had been 16,000 before earthquake. (There are 2,500 now.) So it was possible to open such a place in the expectation of getting local business. Tourism in those days meant a few people coming back from Athens in July or August. Dimitris says, 'Maybe we would have ten tourists in a year, then next year there might be twenty – we would say 100% up!'

Lula says she has heard stories from her Grandma of the place being full of local people coming for lunch, some of them swimming over from the town.

Dimitris himself went to sea as a young man. For four or five years he worked on merchant ships like many Greek men, flying back to work at the taverna in the summer.

'I became a Second Mate but then I gave it up and anchored here. I did my trips and saw what I wanted to see. Ithaca is too small to spend the whole of your youth; you need to travel and come back like in Cavathy's poem. Do you know the other poem by him? When you are young you see the bright lights of candles ahead of you, but when you look back.– you see smoke! But if global warming makes the sea level rise you'll find me just up there, fishing.'

Dimitris talks about the early flotillas with nostalgia.

'Some of the flotilla staff stayed for maybe five years. They got to know everybody, and seemed like part of the family. People were very sad to leave the Ionian. One year there was a big party in Abelike Bay for the staff who were leaving that year. I'll tell you what I want you to say in your book – all the bloody old skippers and lead-crews should come down and have a flotilla together. I'd leave this place and go round with them! Even the ones from Australia and New Zealand would come back – my eucalyptus trees remind them of home.'

The first flotillas preferred to anchor off in this corner as it was cooler and more sheltered, though in a big south wind they went next to the ferry boat in town. There was nothing to tie up to down here though – trees and small rocks extended down to the water, as they still do for a good part of this end of the harbour. At one point Dimitris built some small wooden pontoons, and it still rankles that he had to pay the port police for the use of them.

For a short while in the early 1990s the big ferries used this corner while the main quay and the street were under repair; that is the origin of the huge mooring buoy that remains there and the big bollards on the eastern corner of the quay, together with the sloping concrete structure the bollards sit on, which was built for the ferries.

The next step was to have involved using concrete blocks, maybe 12 feet square. These blocks lined the road to town in 1992; subsequently they were placed in the water next to the now unused ferry quay, where they sank into the harbour bottom. Finally EU money built the present quay; the concrete work was ready in 2001, in time for a political candidate to arrive on it by helicopter, covering everyone in gravel. The lights and other services arrived a little later.

This was one of the first harbours locally to be equipped with services for boats, but they are now in a state of disrepair. I don't know if the water has ever been connected, but the visiting boats have played their part in demolishing the boxes for electrical power: big motorboats have backed into them with their extended hydraulic landing ladders, and boats have been moored to them and pulled them out of the quay. Recently someone moored to a lamp post one evening and pulled it into the sea. He then dragged it out of the water by hand – 15 minutes later, the power for the lights would have been on!

Gregory's restaurant, situated at the end of the new quay closest to the town, is also remembered by those on the early flotillas. He is another person who says the old days were the best, but 'I've been twenty-seven years here, and my daughter will be carrying on. Gregory does good food, good prices, same for everybody.'

# Kioni

Denham's guides, published in the early 1970s, call Kioni a delightful sheltered bay but suggest mooring 'stern-to on the quay on the NE side of the creek' or anchoring 'near the head of the creek. – there is barely room for two yachts to swing.' The excellent photograph in his book shows clearly that there was then no mole extending from the north-east side. This, together with modifications to the quay itself, has transformed the space available for visiting boats. Mike Cox's survey notes say that in 1976 the water was too shallow to lie at the quay.

All the same, the photos here show that Kioni has changed much less than many of the Ionian

> **H**ammond Innes: 'Kioni – a steep little place with just enough room to swing between rock and quay. By the time we had finished lunch, in a bare little shack that did service as an estiatorion, the wind had followed us round and was blowing hard into the harbour. We left in a hurry, our anchor dragging on the rocky bottom.'
>
> **Lawrence Durrell:** 'The holidaymaker … will have the most pleasure if he rents a little boat at Port Snow (Hioni) and paddles among the rocky headlands.'

ports. The pair of pictures looking along the quay show the buildings easily identifiable: the little wooden jetty is longer now, and there is a more permanent roof on the taverna, but otherwise the main change is that the boats are bigger. The angle of the photos does not show the mole, which now extends at right-angles to the main quay, or that it had not been built when the 1978 photo was taken.

In the 1970s there were two tavernas – the one with a straw roof run by the 'old men', and the Avra Restaurant at the head of the bay, which is still in the same family. Kostas, who can be found at the Avra preparing cutlery at 9.00am and taking orders till late at night, remembers when they had only five or six tables down on the quay. Now there can easily be eighty boats in the harbour during the high summer, including those moored off. I was told by a local man that on 14 August 2007 there were 147 boats there; the precise date he gave may seem like circumstantial evidence, but the number suggests that it should have been possible to walk across the bay dry-footed.

Now there are several interesting restaurants, but in addition to the mini-market, which used to be known as the Shop that Sells Everything, and the jewellers right by the harbour, there are now craft-shops and a jewellery workshop where the building itself is almost as interesting as the skills and artefacts on display. This growth has taken place without endangering the style and atmosphere of the village, and most of the businesses are locally based.

Kioni in 1994 (*above*) and 2007 – a second look is required to see which is which. *Kevan Dearman/Author*

*Left and above* The view towards
Kostas's restaurant in 1994, and a
similar view in 2007.
*Kevan Dearman/Author*

Mike Cox's 1976 survey notes for
Port Kioni. *YCA*

*Opposite* The first photo was taken in 1978 for the YCA brochure, and was headed 'Kioni: Ionian Fishing Village'. Some of the houses are in better order in 2007, but otherwise the village is remarkably unchanged.
*YCA/Bernard Jakeways*

*This page* Hamilton House at the end of the quay. The shot with no boats is from 1994 and shows the construction of the pathway then – the later picture was taken in 2007. *Kevan Dearman/ Bernard Jakeways*

# Pera Pigahdi and other small anchorages

Ithaca's harbours with services for the boats have naturally become the favourites for flotillas as well as private boats. Vathi and Kioni are nowadays busy places, and so is Frikes, which was little used at first but whose welcoming restaurants nowadays attract visitors despite the inefficient floating jetty. However, the yachtsmen of the 1950s and '60s include references to a number of other possible anchorages, which to this day are very underused as overnight stops. This is partly explained by looking at the popular tourist maps of the time, which give these bays more prominence than the shelter they provide or the space available to anchor in reasonably shallow water.

Doug Kennett and his family enjoyed Sarakiniko Cove (see the photo on page 11), and Port Andreas in the south is mentioned by Bradford – 'One of the most lovely bays and inlets of Ithaca' – and Innes – 'Open to the south-east, looked distinctly inhospitable'. Mike Cox visited it too on his survey, saying that it was 'not as pleasant as Denham suggests – the beach is very small and is really only suitable for 1 or 2 yachts'.

Pera Pigahdi was a popular swim-stop from the earliest flotillas. In 1981 Prince Charles was on honeymoon in Greece on *Britannia*. A flotilla sailing down the coast of Ithaca saw *Britannia* pass, and there was much waving and dipping of ensigns. Later on, when they were swimming at Pera Pigahdi, they saw the Royal Yacht appearing round the southern corner of Ithaca and anchoring in the bay. A launch was lowered, which motored shoreward – Charles and Diana had obviously agreed with them that this was the perfect place to swim.

Barrie Neilson

# 15
# Cephalonia

## Fiscardo

Mike Cox deals only briefly with Fiscardo, and this is the only reference to Cephalonia in his notes, although he surveyed mainland ports and the Dragonera islands in some detail. For a number of years this island was beyond the range of the flotilla companies.

> 'I called very briefly here on the ferry en route to Ithaca. The harbour looks pleasant and is at the moment being extended and the inner basin developed. This could make it a useful flotilla stop – however, locals on the ferry did talk about very strong winds indeed between Ithaca and Cephalonia.'

The 1978 YCA brochure shows Fiscardo on the chart, but not in the text describing the flotilla route.

Among the many bars and restaurants around the harbour now, Tassos of The Captain's Cabin is the undisputed elder statesman. Because the early Ionian flotillas were using Corfu airport, and ports north of Levkas were their bases, Fiscardo was a long way south for many of the boats, and while the northern harbours prospered and those on Levkas and Ithaca were regularly visited by flotillas, Fiscardo might see one flotilla in six weeks.

Tassos went to an end-of-season party at Gouvia for the flotilla crews and told them, 'Fiscardo is beautiful – I'll arrange showers, cocktails, breakfast, and space on quay.' It was this action that brought Fiscardo into the routes for the boats, prepared the village for the expansion south when Preveza airport opened, and led eventually to Fiscardo's

> *H*ammond **Innes:** 'Fiscardon … is prettier, a half-circle of white houses reflected in quiet water.'

place at the centre of the economy of the north of Cephalonia.

In those days The Captain's Cabin was the 'only bar and patisserie, with breakfasts' – there was one other restaurant, a more traditional Greek place. The food has changed; in the old days people used to complain it was too heavy. Tassos says that everywhere in the area Greek kitchens now use better-quality materials. Visitors always ask for Greek food when they first arrive, but now there is a variety available including Italian or even Thai dishes.

Despite the number of boats that moor, or try to moor, every day, there is plenty of pressure in the town to keep Fiscardo from the sort of growth that would spoil its traditional character. The original quay stretched round to where the floating pontoon is, though as the early photos show it has since been extended and made easier to use. The pontoon faced opposition in the mid-1990s, but apart from recent improvements to the wall on the north side, where boats can take long lines ashore, and changes to road traffic regulations and the ferry terminal, which keep big vehicles out of the main part of the village, no substantial changes have been made to the harbour and there are no plans to make more boat spaces.

In any case, says Tassos, if there were more spaces there would just be more motorboats, though rising fuel costs have cut the numbers of these, even of the Greek-owned boats. He says that he is nostalgic for the early days because of the people, and still

*Above* Fiscardo in 1976: Doug Kennett's yacht and a fishing-boat are the only ones on the quay, and the crews of the two boats were the only people in the taverna, where 'we had a fresh lobster and our children had jumbo prawns straight off the boat'. *Doug Kennett*

*Below* Fiscardo in 1980. *YCA*

*Above* A 1982 article in *Yachting World* refers to Fiscardo as 'a sleepy haven with just two tavernas'. *Noel Cash*

*Below* Another view of Fiscardo in 1982: a flotilla is double-mooring because most of the quay was not yet appropriate for yachts. *R. Jones*

counts some of the early skippers amongst his close friends. Then skippers and clients saw sailing as a sport, in small boats. 'Now they want big boats with two toilets, showers, double beds.' He points out that one of the early companies went under because they were offering boats that were too big – Sadler 29s or 32s! 'The boats on the quay now make the early boats look like dinghies.' Whatever the size of boats he prefers 'Balanced people, down-to-earth, not tycoons.'

As well as being the relaxed host at The Captain's Cabin, Tassos is a shrewd and practical businessman with a broad view of the island's economy. He points out that the north part of the island with expensive transport links has to attract people with a 'better wallet', and to cater for them the people in the shops and restaurants have to dress well and treat them well. He is a director of Ionian Island Holidays, which brings close to 14,000 people each year to Cephalonia.

'All to top accommodation. There are other companies too – small, but quality. All benefit … the man who sells pigs, eggs, chickens, the grocer, the carpenter, the blacksmith. They are not worried it is not traditional. Traditional things are there too, but there is a little money-making machine. I was the first one catering for tourists; we had the first brandy glasses, scrambled eggs, bacon and eggs. Little things make a difference. The villages are doing better too – local people with luxury villas and pools for letting.'

There are fewer fishing boats now. Fish is bought from Ithacan boats, or boats from Argostili or Levkas. The local fishermen are making a living, says Tassos, but there are fewer fish than twenty years ago; the alternative to small-time fishing is to be very professional, which means the big trawlers, which drag up everything in the sea.

The change in the harbour can clearly be seen from Ian Meikle's story on page 60 of windsurfing there in 1983; there were no port authorities, and not much traffic. Now there are four or five ferries in the summer, together with bigger tripper boats.

Jack Noutch

# 16
## Paleros

Paleros has featured in the flotilla routes since very early on. During the early 1980s the companies experimented with the town for changeovers once Preveza airport came into use, though Levkas, Nidri and eventually Sivota became more popular.

However, the town has a life of its own quite separate from the tourist trade, so the harbour and other facilities for visiting boats sometimes seem to be incidental. Of course, this is one of its attractions: no one wants to bring a yacht to a theme park. It does mean, however, that the town is a 'best-kept secret' even though the Sunsail Vounaki base has been built just down the bay.

The harbour was largely destroyed in the last war, since the invading forces thought it might have strategic importance. For a long time local people faced the danger of being killed by mines remaining from the fortifications. When Mike Cox made his survey in 1976 the harbour was just a stump. Subsequently the main arm of the present harbour was built, the stones along the outside of the wall being placed there for ballast to protect it.

Paleros harbour in early May 2002. There is some space, but many of these boats are settling down for the season. *Author*

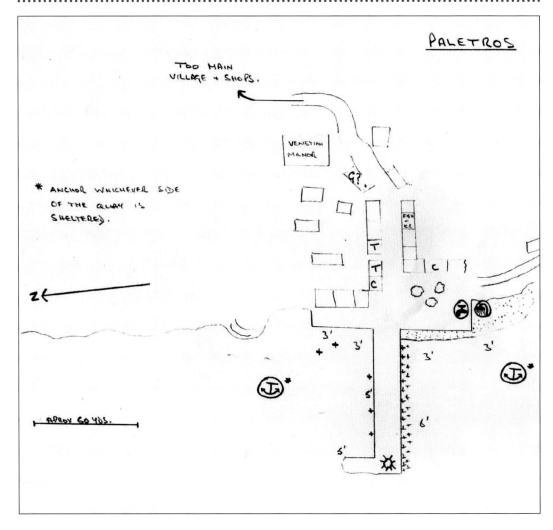

Mike Cox's sketch from 1976: the harbour had still not been rebuilt
since the war. 'Anchor whichever side of the quay is sheltered.' *YCA*

Quite recently the little floating jetty was added. There is currently a plan to build another pontoon, 50 metres to the north.

So the town has decent shelter, good shops for provisions, excellent restaurants, free water, even a bathing beach. Why does it remain on the edge of the flotilla routes?

One reason may be a concern about finding space. For a number of years OCC based its boats here, and empty yachts were moored in the corner of the harbour. A handsome building by the harbour still bears the OCC initials even though the company is now based at Corfu. In addition Paleros seems to have become the home port for a good many private boats, some of them empty for much of the season.

For whatever reason it is not always possible to count on finding a place in the harbour, and the number of free spaces is rarely sufficient to bring in a flotilla. Year after year local people discuss ways to encourage the 'mince-eaters' to move on, and year after year nothing dramatic happens. The fishermen are OK, the farmers are OK, and the restaurant owners are doing well too, with more Greek people discovering the village as a holiday destination.

So maybe Paleros hasn't got the balance too far wrong, and we visitors in yachts should just enjoy being able to share the town on its own terms.

# Index